Sharing Authority in the Museum

Sharing Authority in the Museum provides a detailed and fully contextualised study of a heritage assemblage over time, from the mid-nineteenth century to the present day. Focussing on Māori objects, predominantly originating from the Ngā Paerangi tribe, housed in Oxford's Pitt Rivers Museum, the book examines the nuances of cross-cultural interactions between an indigenous community and an anthropological museum.

Analysis centres on the legacy of historic ethnographic collecting on indigenous communities and museums, and the impact of different value systems and world views on access to heritage objects. Questions of curatorial responsibilities and authority over access rights are explored. Proposing a method for indigenous engagement to address this legacy, and making recommendations to guide participants when forging relationships based around indigenous cultural heritage, Michelle Horwood shows how to negotiate power and authority within these assemblages. She argues that by doing this and acknowledging and communicating our difficult histories, together we can move from collaborative approaches to shared authority and indigenous self-determination, progressing the task of decolonising the museum.

Addressing a salient, complex issue by way of a grounded case study, *Sharing Authority in the Museum* is key reading for museum practitioners working with ethnographic collections, as well as scholars and students working in the fields of museum, heritage, Indigenous or cultural studies. It should also be of great interest to indigenous communities wishing to take the lessons learned from Ngā Paerangi's experiences further within their own spheres of museum engagement.

Michelle Horwood is a teacher, scholar and museum curator. She has worked extensively in the heritage sector as a curator, archaeologist and researcher, where connecting communities with their heritage has been the primary focus of her professional practice.

Museums in Focus

Series Editor: Kylie Message

Committed to the articulation of big, even risky, ideas in small format publications, 'Museums in Focus' challenges authors and readers to experiment with, innovate, and press museums and the intellectual frameworks through which we view these. It offers a platform for approaches that radically rethink the relationships between cultural and intellectual dissent and crisis and debates about museums, politics and the broader public sphere.

'Museums in Focus' is motivated by the intellectual hypothesis that museums are not innately 'useful,' 'safe' or even 'public' places, and that recalibrating our thinking about them might benefit from adopting a more radical and oppositional form of logic and approach. Examining this problem requires a level of comfort with (or at least tolerance of) the idea of crisis, dissent, protest and radical thinking, and authors might benefit from considering how cultural and intellectual crisis, regeneration and anxiety have been dealt with in other disciplines and contexts.

Recently published titles:

Museums and Racism
Kylie Message

Sharing Authority in the Museum
Distributed objects, reassembled relationships
Michelle Horwood

https://www.routledge.com/Routledge-Museums-in-Focus/book-series/RMIF

⌐MUSEUMS IN FOCUS⌐

Logo by James Verdon (2017)

Anonymous graffiti, Athens. Image and logo by James Verdon (2017).

Sharing Authority in the Museum

Distributed Objects, Reassembled Relationships

Michelle Horwood

Routledge
Taylor & Francis Group

LONDON AND NEW YORK

First published 2019 by Routledge

2 Park Square, Milton Park, Abingdon, Oxfordshire OX14 4RN

52 Vanderbilt Avenue, New York, NY 10017

Routledge is an imprint of the Taylor & Francis Group, an informa business

First issued in paperback 2020

British Library Cataloguing-in-Publication Data
A catalogue record for this book is available from the British Library

Library of Congress Cataloging-in-Publication Data
A catalog record for this book has been requested

ISBN: 978-0-8153-6993-6 (hbk)
ISBN: 978-0-367-60661-9 (pbk)

Typeset in Times New Roman
by Apex CoVantage, LLC

For John, Henry and Mackenzie

Contents

Illustrations

Acknowledgements

This book started out as a germ of an idea for PhD research to crystallise the powerful impact my experiences as a museum curator, working with Māori communities and their material heritage in Whanganui, had on my professional practice, and I am grateful to many people for helping with its development. My greatest and heartfelt thanks go to my family – to my mother Margaret, my sister Nicola, my husband John, and sons Henry and Mackenzie, and remembering my father Basil – without whose support and encouragement this book would not have been possible.

For all those who participated in and supported my research, thank you for providing me with access to your communities and collections, for permission to share your words, mātauranga and taonga, and for your openness, generosity, hospitality and kindness. In particular I acknowledge Ngā Paerangi people past and present. I will be forever grateful to you for walking this path with me and supporting my exploration of your heritage. I would especially like to thank Ken Clarke, Hera Pēina, Haimona Rzoska, Morvin Simon whānau and Katrina Hāwira for welcoming me so warmly into your world and giving of your time and knowledge so generously. Also the Ngā Paerangi team who travelled to Oxford with me – Hera, Haimona, Katrina, Wīpaki Peeti, Luana Tawaroa, Takahia Tawaroa, Teresa Peeti, Ereti Wisneski and Tuata Angus – and to the wider community for making their travel possible.

I extend a huge thank you to Dr Conal McCarthy for his sustained intellectual engagement in and enthusiasm for my work. Also Dr Laura Peers for her support, and that of her colleagues at Pitt Rivers Museum. Thanks also to my past colleagues at Whanganui Regional Museum, and present friends, in particular Sharon Dell, for starting this ball rolling, and Libby Sharpe and Sandi Black for access to collections and records. To my colleagues and students at Toihoukura, thank you for providing insights into the benefits of dual knowledge systems, for continuing to teach me about the value of community, and for your patience with my many mistakes as I navigate your world.

Introduction

In 2006 the director of the Whanganui Regional Museum, Sharon Dell, while exploring the recently launched online database of the Pitt Rivers Museum, discovered a large collection of taonga Māori (treasured Māori objects) that appeared to originate from a Whanganui settler, Charles Smith. The museum's trust board received this information with particular interest as one member of the board was a direct descendant of the chief, Takarangi, who was the source of much of the material Smith had collected, and another, Ken Clarke, was a local tribal historian who lived at Kaiwhāiki where Smith had farmed. Thus begins a narrative that will embrace a relational assemblage of people, places, events and things that span nearly two centuries and 19,000 kilometres, and which is the focus of this book.

> The post-colonial museum is fundamentally about inverting power relations and the voice of authority.
>
> Christina Kreps (2011, p. 75)

This is a book about the centrality of relationships in contemporary museum practice for meaningful museum-indigenous community engagement, in particular when distance is a factor. My intention is to describe the different perceptions of objects as physical manifestations of social relationships and, through a detailed, situated case study, how this might foster enduring relationships between indigenous originating communities and the museum-based custodians of their cultural patrimony.

In New Zealand, and other post-colonial settler nations such as Australia and Canada, the democratisation of museum practice for indigenous collections has been one outcome of the political presence and power of indigenous peoples and the assertion of indigenous autonomy, as well as the proximity of indigenous communities and museums. This has empowered varying degrees of self-determination for traditional owners in the management of their heritage collections. Innovative practice in museology and related fields has therefore differed from elsewhere as a result of the need for negotiated relationships with indigenous communities and recognition of indigenous authority. In New Zealand, acknowledgement of Māori epistemological frameworks and authority over cultural heritage has resulted in effective Māori participation within museums at governance and operational levels and in the application of practices, specific to individual communities, for the cultural safety of taonga Māori,[1] staff and visitors. This has been happening in New Zealand museums for several decades (C. Clarke, 2002; Johnstone, 2006; McCarthy, 2011; Mead, 1986; Tamarapa, n.d.), but has not always been the case elsewhere. In some museums in England, although strategies are employed to engage with the indigenous communities from whom the ethnographic material in their care originated (Krmpotich, Peers, with the Haida Repatriation Committee, & staff of the Pitt Rivers Museum and British Museum, 2013; Lythberg, Hogsden, & Ngata, 2017; Peers & Brown, 2009; Thomas, Adams, Lythberg, Nuku, & Salmond, 2016), there appears to be a reluctance to move beyond this practice and embed these strategies in institutional policy.

Furthermore, although this decolonised museology has been manifest for several decades, I have observed through my experience as a museum curator working with communities, that originating communities[2] still fail to access their cultural heritage housed in museums *at distance* when they have no affiliation with academic or other cultural institutions which can facilitate contact and communication, and because they are often disadvantaged in terms of resources. Moreover, the lack of online collection databases until recently made finding objects difficult. Significantly, ethnographic museums are also constrained by the scope and scale of their collections, resource limitations, institutional priorities, and, in some cases, a lack of desire to work with originating communities.

This raises a number of questions central to contemporary museum practice. Who can access museum collections and who decides? What is the true legacy of ethnographic collecting for museums and what responsibilities do the current custodians of these collections have to their originating communities? These questions, important for museums and museum anthropology, remain largely unanswered. In this book I shall respond to these questions and add to our knowledge and understanding of these issues by examining a network assemblage comprising a collector and his collection, a Māori community and an English museum, through time and across space, to explore the impact of different knowledge systems on access to heritage objects in the present. In this chapter I provide an overview of the pertinent literature and the theoretical framework – assemblage theory[3] – which is applied to the network of events and effects falling out of the in-depth analysis of a specific case study, as well as an outline of subsequent chapters.

At the core of the issue considered here are the difficulties that originating communities have in accessing their cultural heritage in museums that are geographically remote, engaging in face-to-face interactions and establishing *ongoing* relationships with the institutional custodians of this heritage. In this book I suggest that the analysis of the different cultural perspectives and knowledge systems of a Māori tribal community and an English museum community to enable the meanings of a group of heritage items to both groups, over time, to be better understood, will help to show how ongoing relationships can be developed between them. From this, I propose ways and means for indigenous groups to negotiate relationships with museums that hold collections of their ancestral heritage when they are geographically remote from these collections.

I achieve this by specifically analysing the relationships between three constituent parts of this network, a collector of indigenous heritage items and his collection now housed in a museum in England: the Charles Smith collection; Ngā Paerangi: a Māori tribal community in New Zealand who are the customary owners of many items in this collection; and the Pitt Rivers Museum: the current custodians of the collection. The outcomes of the recent reconnection of these components contributes to this analysis. This is a significant contribution to the field in which the research is situated, namely museum studies and, in particular, to the community engagement work that is such a feature of current professional practice. These findings, combined with my own museum experience and with developments in museum practice, provide clarity on the meaning of heritage objects for specific communities. This book builds on literature exploring relationship-building between museums and indigenous communities, specifically that of Krmpotich and Peers (2013), Onciul (2015) and Isaac (2015) relating to community engagement. It makes a contribution to the field through highlighting the efficacy of factors that impact on relationships over time and space, namely power and values. Emerging out of this research, I develop an argument which identifies new ways and means for indigenous and museum communities to interact, articulate why this is beneficial for both communities, and how this can progress museological responsibilities in the early twenty-first century. I focus on understanding the impact of different ontologies on social relations with heritage items, while endorsing the contention that museums have a moral imperative to grant indigenous communities control over representation and access to their tangible and intangible heritage.

Setting the scene

I will now take a closer look at the general research context and the issues in contemporary museum practice and indigenous engagement with museum-held heritage that motivated this research. One manifestation of a new museology within Western museum practice over the past several decades has been enhanced community engagement with museums. This has not always been an equitable process with, as I argue here, difficulties of access for communities located remotely from their heritage in museum collections. An increasing body of literature is exploring the ways in which museums are seeking to engage with indigenous communities (Bolton, Thomas, Bonshek, Adams, & Burt, 2013; Herle, 2003; Isaac, 2009, 2015; Muntean, Hennessy, Matkin, Rowley, & Wilson, 2017; Muntean, Hennessy, Matkin, Rowley, & Wilson, 2017; Peers & Brown, 2003; Rowley, 2014), and the need to move beyond the asymmetry of the contact zone model through shared authority (Boast, 2011; Onciul, 2015). While geographical distance has provided challenges for initiating, developing and maintaining relationships between museums and indigenous communities, these challenges are often used as opportunities for development (Bolton, 2003; de Stecher & Loyer, 2009; Fienup-Riordan, 2003; Hakiwai, 1995; Hennessy et al., 2013; Krmpotich et al., 2013; Lythberg et al., 2017; Peers & Brown, 2003), although bearing in mind Marstine's (2011a, p. 5) observation that in "museums today creativity and risk taking are often funnelled through one-off projects." There is extensive literature on collaborations between museums and indigenous communities (for example, Allen & Hamby, 2011; Bolton et al., 2013; Gadoua, 2010; Hafner, 2010; Krmpotich et al., 2013; Nightingale & Swallow, 2003; Peers & Brown, 2016; Raymond & Salmond, 2008; Thomas et al., 2016). While a range of strategies for engaging with indigenous communities has been tested by museums, comprehensively articulated by contributors in Peers and Brown's (2003) authoritative volume *Museums and Source Communities*, few have been community led (Bolton et al., 2013; Isaac, 2009, 2015; Krmpotich et al., 2013; Lythberg et al., 2017; Peers & Brown, 2016; Potaka & Butts, 2003). Furthermore, few studies have documented the 'difficulties and complexities' of museum-community engagement (Krmpotich et al., 2013; Onciul, 2015). I address these issues in this book.

Non-western knowledge systems and ways of being

> The single most important aspect of an indigenous world view is the notion that the world is alive, conscious and flowing with a perennial energy. The natural world is not so much the repository of wisdom as wisdom itself, flowing with purpose and design.
>
> Te Ahukaramū Charles Royal (2003, p. 44)

Acknowledgement of the validity of different knowledge systems and the values that guide our interactions in the world has led to a number of inspiring initiatives around museum-held indigenous heritage (Lonetree, 2012;

Mignolo, 2009). As Clavir (2002 after Swentzell (1991)) suggests, central to an appropriate museology in the twenty-first century is the identification of differences as well as commonalities in value systems between indigenous people and museums, and methods to bridge the cultural distance between them.

A central premise of this book is that taking into account epistemological and ontological differences will improve understanding of the past and present life of heritage items for indigenous communities and museums. Epistemological and ontological perspectives as well as value systems develop through cultural identity and experiences in the world. A theme considered by Kreps (2003, p. 3) when she stated that "it's no longer sufficient to treat indigenous objects as inert relics" and that "taking into account different indigenous practices and interests serves to decentre the dominance of scientifically based museology." Acknowledging disparate knowledge systems enables consideration to be given to the different meanings for communities, and the roles within them, that heritage objects may have.[4]

Furthermore, a major tenet of anthropology and a central tenet of this book, as A. Clarke (2014, p. 18) describes, is "that lines between persons and things can vary by culture." For example, Hays-Gilpin and Lomatewama (2013) discuss objects for Hopi in the US as "animate in the sense, that they are part of the flow of life in a meshwork of relationships" (ibid., p. 266). They are thus 'living' in a specific sense where human-like requirements such as 'feeding' are analogous to Māori ontological perspectives of 'keeping taonga warm' (McKenzie, 1993). To recognise the animacy of objects and thereby consider their relationships with the world rather than the nomenclatural classification within which they fit, broadens our thinking when we are responsible for museum collections, and expedites the development of sensitive approaches for the care of and access to collections. Correspondingly, recognition of the knowledge and expertise of museum professionals as equally relevant and meaningful within their own contexts to that of indigenous people, and that both perspectives are equally valid, as Muñoz (2009, p. 13) states, "aids the process of democratizing knowledge as well as access to it." Here I acknowledge the validity of different knowledge and attendant values systems and identify the specific benefits of each for a collection of heritage items, and whether a focussed and detailed study of the relationships these items generate can result in more than a one-off project for a museum and a community.

Museum ethics

Two further key issues important for any exploration of museum-indigenous community relationships are access (or participation) and contemporary museum ethics. In Marstine's (2011b) volume, recontextualising the discourse on the new museum ethics, she explores three museological themes for moral agency: social inclusion embracing democracy and diversity, radical transparency acknowledging accountability, and shared guardianship of heritage to provide "an ethics of sustainability, not accumulation" (2011a, p. 19). In the same volume Kreps (2011, p. 75) discusses the decolonising of Western museums requiring the inverting of power relations and the voice of authority. I have quoted Kreps at the beginning of this chapter to indicate the centrality of this principle here. The importance of equal and two-way relationships between museums and stakeholders is not a new concept (for example, Bestermen, 2006; Boast, 2011 citing Clifford, 1997; Poignant & Poignant, 1996). Furthermore, Whaanga (2012) discusses the importance of identifying appropriate customary practice and ethics when working with indigenous collections to ensure the integrity of the collection is maintained and contextualisation of the collection is possible. These themes have particular relevance to the present study.

Assemblages

A theoretical lens can be also be useful to provide a framework for the analysis of a network of events and effects and to describe values in analyses of social life, particularly where cross-cultural research takes into account different value systems.

I have drawn on assemblage theory as means to connect humans and things across time and space. Assemblages as they relate to bodies as a means of analysing societal complexity, first defined by Deleuze and Guattari (1987, p. 90), and developed further by De Landa (2006, 2016), has been used by Bennett (2010, p. 202) specifically in terms of the history of relations between the colonised and coloniser and the development of 'indigenous governmentality' in twentieth-century Australia. Bennett and Healy's volume *Assembling Culture* similarly explores how culture "is assembled by bringing together heterogeneous elements (artefacts, people, texts, architecture, etcetera) and organising these into distinctly configured relations to one another" (Bennett & Healy, 2011, p. 2).

Marcus and Saka (2006) discuss assemblage, with regard to ethnographic anthropology, as it has been used as a structure to describe values (including emergence, heterogeneity, the decentred and the ephemeral) in descriptions and analyses of social life. Considering assemblage theory in terms of the "always-emergent conditions of the present" as a means to analyse the contemporary (ibid., pp. 101–102), has specific relevance to this investigation of notions of 'value' or difference of value systems as well as the nature of relationships between museums and originating communities in contemporary society. The use of assemblage as a 'time-limited' (ibid., p. 102) theory has particular appeal for an analysis which embraces temporal and spatial parameters in a range of ways in relation to analysing the interrelatedness and/or interactions of the different object and human relations, and their reassembly. However, a word of warning from De Landa seems apt when considering the fragmented nature of assemblages in this context and the need to find practical ways in which to reassemble them. He writes, "The identity of any assemblage at any level of scale is always the product of a process . . . and it is always precarious, since other processes . . . can destabilize it" (De Landa, 2006, p. 28). In this book a practical approach to reassembling these fragments will be described.

Harrison (2013, p. 20ff) attests to the salience of the application of the assemblage metaphor which I have found similarly useful. Firstly, considering an assemblage as a group of artefacts found together representing a particular activity at a point in time and place, they employed taphonomic processes borrowed from archaeological analysis to provide new ways to understand museum collection formation. Similarly, Kirshenblatt-Gimblett (1998) has used the metaphor of assemblage in relation to the fragmentary nature of ethnographic museum collections. Harrison (2013, p. 23) also describes the analysis of a collection by multiple experts as a 'reassembling' as it draws not only objects but people and objects together.

Assemblage theory is therefore useful for developing a model to bring together Ngā Paerangi iwi, the Charles Smith collection and the Pitt Rivers Museum. Its usefulness lies in its application to the coloniser–colonised relationships, by providing a framework for the case study that will assist with the formation of contemporary, museum-community relationships.

In this study, assemblages can be material or social and comprise all, but not only, the following components – people, things, places, organisations, institutional policies, knowledge systems, events, actions, state/indigenous politics – and these are temporally and spatially contingent. Assemblages are considered analysable, as they have the ability to be broken down into their constituent parts, or disassembled, so that these can be considered separately, and then reconstructed from these parts, or reassembled (Harrison, 2013). Components can be extracted from one assemblage and inserted into another where their relations may be different. For this study, which involves building relationships between two contemporary groups – one a tribal community in a former settler colony, the other an academic institution and museum within the colonising society, framed around a collection of historical heritage items – this framework is useful in terms of the interactions of the heritage items with the institution and with the community over time and space, where different knowledge and attendant value systems create different meanings and relationships. The result is contingent and, as Macdonald (2011, p. 137) states, "inevitably partial – [as] it is never possible to follow all of the chains of connections that might be involved." For this study nonetheless, this disassembling can be reassembled by drawing objects and people together to create benefits for the community, museum and the collection in the present. It will also reveal the effects of the agency of heritage items, leadership change, relations of power, and organisational priorities on things such as contemporary museum practice, indigene–museum interactions and the revitalisation of cultural processes.

To summarise, the democratisation of museum practice for indigenous collections has been one outcome of the proximity of indigenous communities and museums and has resulted in empowering varying degrees of self-determination for traditional owners in the management of their heritage collections. There are a number of reasons why indigenous communities have difficulty accessing their cultural heritage when it is housed in museums *at distance*, and I argue that this study is important because there is little *ongoing* indigene–museum engagement where geographic distance isolates these groups from one another. I suggest that a new approach to investigating indigene–museum relationships where distance is a factor is through the application of a theoretical model to a detailed, situated case study over time, comparing and contrasting cultural perspectives. I argue that the analysis of the different cultural perspectives and knowledge systems of a tribal and a museum community will enable the meanings of a group of indigenous heritage items to both groups, over time, to be better understood. This will contribute to the development of ongoing relationships between them. This book will add to the emerging body of writing that is re-evaluating the way in which these communities interact by documenting some of the 'difficulties and complexities' of museum–community engagement, and the mechanisms whereby 'true democratic exchange' can occur in relationships between them (Lynch & Alberti, 2010, p. 20).

Sharing Authority comprises three parts: the background or research context, the disassembly reassembly of the heritage network, and the implications for museum practice. Chapter 1 focuses upon the specific case study communities, introducing the collector, indigenous culture and community, and museum. Using assemblage theory, these three components – Charles Smith and his dispersed collection, Ngā Paerangi iwi (tribe) the source of much of this collection, and the Pitt Rivers Museum the current custodian of the collection – are disassembled providing a brief history of indigene–settler relations in New Zealand during the nineteenth century at the time and place the collection was developed framed within an anthropological lens of museum evolution in England and New Zealand during the same period.

The second chapter brings the narrative into the present day unfolding a museum encounter with Ngā Paerangi iwi members travelling to Oxford to reconnect with their ancestral heritage at the Pitt Rivers Museum and meet the staff responsible for its care. Chapter 3 runs through emergent themes of the disassembly, disentangling and reassembling of the disparate parts of this historical-contemporary network identifying the different actors, agencies and elements of the assemblage across time and through space in the context of this particular collection and historical context. Chapter 4 considers the insight that an understanding of the disparate cultural perspectives of assemblage components will have to the past and present lives of the tangible heritage at the centre of this research. It outlines the indigenous engagement praxis that emerged from the disassembly-reassembly described in Chapter 3. Finally, the conclusion returns to the questions about museum practice and the implications for museum–indigenous community relationships with which the book began. It considers where to from here for the future of indigenous authority for museum-held collections.

Notes

1 Taonga Māori in this case specifically refers to tangible ancestral heritage items and their associated intangible qualities such as historical narratives, referred to hereafter as taonga.
2 Source communities is a term often used for the communities from whom indigenous material heritage originated. Defined by Peers and Brown (2003, p. 2) to refer "both to these groups in the past when artefacts were collected, as well as to their descendants today." This term, in relation to museum collections, is going out of favour as it implies the one-way source of material heritage and associated intangible qualities removed or studied by museums, collectors and anthropologists, rather than suggesting relationships and continuity. I prefer to use the term originating communities.
3 In recent museum studies scholarship assemblage theory is being drawn on by scholars to provide a theoretical basis in the reconceptualisation of heritage as heterogeneous assemblages of people and things (Bennett & Healy, 2011; Harrison, Byrne, & Clarke, 2013; Macdonald, 2011).
4 As discussed by Bennett and Healy (2011), Boast (2011), Clarke (2002), Clifford (2004), Henare, Holbraad, and Wastell (2007b), Kreps (2006), Sleeper-Smith (2009), Smith (1999), Tamarapa (n.d.), Tapsell (2006) and Viveiros de Castro (2004), for example.

References

Allen, L., & Hamby, L. (2011). Pathways to knowledge: Research, agency and power relations in the context of collaborations between museums and source communities. In S. Byrne, A. Clarke, R. Harrison, & R. Torrence (Eds.), *Unpacking the collection: Museums, identity and agency* (pp. 209–229). New York: Springer.

Bennett, T. (2010). Making and mobilising worlds: Assembling and governing the other. In T. Bennett & P. Joyce (Eds.), *Material powers: Cultural studies, history and the material turn* (pp. 188–208). London: Routledge.

Bennett, T., & Healy, C. (2011). *Assembling culture*. London: Routledge.

Bestermen, T. (2006). Museum ethics. In S. Macdonald (Ed.), *A companion to museum studies* (Vol. Blackwell companions in cultural studies). Malden, MA: Wiley-Blackwell.

Boast, R. (2011). Neocolonial collaboration: Museum as contact zone revisited. *Museum Anthropology, 34*(1), 56–70.

Bolton, L. (2003). The object in view: Aborigines, Melanesians and museums. In L. L. Peers & A. K. Brown (Eds.), *Museums and source communities: A Routledge reader* (pp. 42–54). London: Routledge.

Bolton, L., Thomas, N., Bonshek, E., Adams, J., & Burt, B. (2013). *Melanesia: Art and encounter*. London: The British Museum Press.

Clarke, A. (2014). Theories of material agency and practice: A guide to collecting urban material culture. *Museum Anthropology, 37*(1), 17–26.

Clarke, C. (2002). Te Ao Turoa: A Maori view of the natural world in Auckland museum. *Te Ara: Journal of Museums Aotearoa, 27*(1), 23–26.

Clavir, M. (2002). *Preserving what is valued: Museums, conservation, and first nations*. Vancouver: University of British Columbia Press.

Clifford, J. (2004). Looking several ways: Anthropology and native heritage in Alaska. *Current Anthropology, 45*(1), 5–30.

De Landa, M. (2006). *A new philosophy of society: Assemblage theory and social complexity*. London: Continuum.

De Landa, M. (2016). *Assemblage theory*. Edinburgh: Edinburgh University Press.

Deleuze, G., & Guattari, F. (1987). *A thousand plateaus: Capitalism and schizophrenia*. London: Continuum.

de Stecher, A., & Loyer, S. (2009). Practising collaborative research: The Great Lakes Research Alliance visits to the Pitt Rivers Museum and British Museum. *Journal of Museum Ethnography, 22*, 145–154.

Fienup-Riordan, A. (2003). Yup'ik Elders in museums: Fieldwork turned on its head. In L. L. Peers & A. K. Brown (Eds.), *Museums and source communities: A Routledge reader* (pp. 28–41). London: Routledge.

Gadoua, M-P. (2010). *The successful collaboration of First Nations, museums and universities: The case of Avataq Cultural Institute, the McCord Museum and McGill University*. Paper presented at the Taking Stock: Museum Studies and Museum Practices in Canada conference, Toronto.

Hafner, D. (2010). Viewing the past through ethnographic collections: Indigenous people and the materiality of images and objects. *Museum History Journal, 3*(2), 257–280.

Hakiwai, A. (1995). Ruatepupuke: Working together, understanding one another. *New Zealand Museums Journal, 25*(1), 42–44.

Harrison, R. (2013). Reassembling ethnographic museum collections. In R. Harrison, S. Byrne, & A. Clarke (Eds.), *Reassembling the collection: Indigenous agency and ethnographic collections* (pp. 3–35). New Mexico: School for Advanced Research (SAR) Press.

Hays-Gilpin, K., & Lomatewama, R. (2013). Curating communities at the Museum of North Arizona. In R. Harrison, S. Byrne, & A. Clarke (Eds.), *Reassembling the collection: Indigenous agency and ethnographic collections* (pp. 259–284). New Mexico: School for Advanced Research (SAR) Press.

Henare, A., Holbraad, M., & Wastell, S. (Eds.). (2007). *Thinking through things: Theorising artefacts in ethnographic perspective.* London: Routledge.

Hennessy, K., Lyons, N., Loring, S., Arnold, C., Joe, M., Elias, A., & Pokiak, J. (2013). The Inuvialuit Living History Project: Digital return as the forging of relationships between institutions, people, and data. *Museum Anthropology Review, 7*(1–2), 44–73.

Herle, A. (2003). Objects, agency and museums: Continuing dialogues between Torres Strait and Cambridge. In L. L. Peers & A. K. Brown (Eds.), *Museums and source communities: A Routledge reader.* London: Routledge.

Isaac, G. (2009). Responsibilities toward knowledge: The Zuni Museum and the reconciling of different knowledge systems. In S. Sleeper-Smith (Ed.), *Contesting knowledge: Museums and indigenous perspectives* (pp. 303–321). Lincoln: University of Nebraska Press.

Isaac, G. (2015). Perclusive alliances: Digital 3-D, museums, and the reconciling of culturally diverse knowledges. *Current Anthropology, 56*(S12), S286–S296.

Johnstone, K. (2006). Mātauranga Māori and museum practice. *He raumi: Resource guides, 31.* Retrieved from www.tepapa.govt.nz/NationalServices/Resources/FundingPlanningManagement/Pages/Biculturaldevelopment.aspx.

Kirshenblatt-Gimblett, B. (1998). *Destination culture: Tourism, museums, and heritage.* Berkeley: University of California Press.

Kreps, C. F. (2003). *Liberating culture: Cross-cultural perspectives on museums, curation and heritage preservation.* London: Routledge.

Kreps, C. F. (2006). Non-western models of museums and curation in cross-cultural perspective. In S. Macdonald (Ed.), *A companion to museum studies* (pp. 457–472). Oxford: Blackwell Publishing.

Kreps, C. F. (2011). Changing the rules of the road: Post-colonialism and the new ethics of museum anthropology. In J. Marstine (Ed.), *Routledge companion to museum ethics: Redefining ethics for the twenty-first century museum* (pp. 70–84). London: Routledge.

Krmpotich, C., Peers, L. L., Haida Repatriation Committee, & Staff of the Pitt Rivers Museum and British Museum. (2013). *This is our life: Haida material heritage and changing museum practice.* Vancouver: University of British Columbia Press.

Lonetree, A. (2012). *Decolonizing museums: Representing Native America in national and tribal museums.* Chapel Hill, NC: University of North Carolina Press.

Lynch, B. T., & Alberti, S. J. M. M. (2010). Legacies of prejudice: Racism, co-production and radical trust in the museum. *Museum Management and Curatorship, 25*(1), 13–35.

Lythberg, B., Hogsden, C., & Ngata, W. (2017). Relational systems and ancient futures: Co-creating a digital contact network in theory and practice. In B. Onciul, M. L. Stefano, & S. Hawke (Eds.), *Engaging heritage, engaging communities* (Vol. Heritage Matters, pp. 205–226). Woodbridge: Boydell Press.

Macdonald, S. (2011). Reassembling Nuremberg, reassembling heritage. In T. Bennett & C. Healy (Eds.), *Assembling culture* (pp. 113–130). London: Routledge.

Marcus, G. E., & Saka, E. (2006). Assemblage. *Theory, Culture & Society, 23*(2–3), 101–106.

Marstine, J. (2011a). The contingent nature of the new museum ethics. In J. Marstine (Ed.), *Routledge companion to museum ethics: Redefining ethics for the twenty-first century museum* (pp. 3–25). London: Routledge.

Marstine, J. (Ed.). (2011b). *Routledge companion to museum ethics: Redefining ethics for the twenty-first century museum.* London: Routledge.

McCarthy, C. (2011). *Museums and Maori: Heritage professionals, indigenous collections, current practice.* Wellington: Te Papa Press.

McKenzie, M. (1993). A challenge to museums – keeping the taonga warm. *Zeitschrift fur Ethnologie, 118,* 79–85.

Mead, S. M. (1986). *Magnificent Te Maori = Te Maori whakahirahira: He korero whakanui i Te Maori.* Auckland: Heinemann.

Mignolo, W. D. (2009). Preface to the report on Niño Korin collection. In A. Muñoz (Ed.), *The power of labelling: Report to Kulturrådet, Arts Council Norway.* Norway: Kulturrådet.

Muñoz, A. (2009). *The power of labelling: Report to Kulturrådet, Arts Council Norway.* Norway: Kulturrådet.

Muntean, R., Hennessy, K., Matkin, B., Rowley, S., & Wilson, J. (2017). *Designing tangible interactions to communicate cultural continuity: ʔeləẃkʷ – Belongings, a tangible table in c̓əsnaʔəm, the city before the city at the Museum of Anthropology.* Paper presented at the Museums and the Web Conference, Cleveland, Ohio. Retrieved from http://mw17.mwconf.org/paper/designing-tangible-interactions-to-communicate-cultural-continuity-%ca%94el%c9%99w%cc%93k%cc%93%ca%b7-belongings-a-tangible-table-in-c%cc%93%c9%99sna%ca%94%c9%99m-the-city-before-the-city/.

Nightingale, E., & Swallow, D. (2003). The arts of the Sikh kingdoms. In L. L. Peers & A. K. Brown (Eds.), *Museums and source communities: A Routledge reader* (pp. 55–71). London: Routledge.

Onciul, B. (2015). *Museums, heritage and indigenous voice: Decolonizing engagement.* New York: Routledge.

Peers, L. L., & Brown, A. K. (Eds.). (2003). *Museums and source communities: A Routledge reader.* London: Routledge.

Peers, L. L., & Brown, A. K. (2009). Colonial photographs and postcolonial relationships: The Kainai-Oxford Photographic Histories Project. In A. M. Timpson (Ed.), *First Nations, first thoughts: The impact of indigenous thought in Canada* (pp. 123–144). Vancouver: University of British Columbia Press.

Peers, L. L., & Brown, A. K. (2016). *Visiting with the ancestors: Blackfoot shirts in museum spaces.* Edmonton: Athabasca University Press.

Poignant, R., & Poignant, A. (1996). *Encounter at Nagalarramba.* Canberra: National Library of Australia.

Potaka, U., & Butts, D. (2003). Ngā taonga tūhono: Treasures that unite people. *Te Ara: Journal of Museums Aotearoa, 20*(2), 4–9.

Raymond, R., & Salmond, A. (2008). *Pasifika styles: Artists inside the museum.* Cambridge: University of Cambridge Museum of Archaeology and Anthropology.

Rowley, S. (2014). The Reciprocal Research Network: The development process. *Museum Anthropology Review, 7*(1–2), 22–43.

Royal, T. A. C. (2003). *The woven universe: Selected writings of Rev. Māori Marsden.* Otaki: Estate of Rev. Māori Marsden.

Sleeper-Smith, S. (2009). *Contesting knowledge: Museums and indigenous perspectives.* Lincoln: University of Nebraska Press.

Smith, L. T. (1999). *Decolonizing methodologies: Research and indigenous peoples.* London: Zed Books.

Swentzell, R. (1991). *Native American vs. Western European philosophy and museum assumptions.* Unpublished planning document for *The Way of the People, Phase I.* National Museum of the American Indian.

Tamarapa, A. (n.d.). *Kaitiakitanga (cultural custodianship) at the Museum of New Zealand Te Papa Tongarewa.* Wellington: Museum of New Zealand Te Papa Tongarewa.

Tapsell, P. (2006). *Ko tawa: Maori treasures of New Zealand.* Auckland: David Bateman.

Thomas, N., Adams, J., Lythberg, B., Nuku, M., & Salmond, A. (Eds.). (2016). *Artefacts of encounter: Cook's voyages, colonial collecting and museum histories.* Dunedin: Otago University Press.

Viveiros de Castro, E. (2004). Exchanging perspectives. The transformation of objects into subjects in Amerindian ontologies: Symposium on the Conciliation of Worldviews: Part 1. *Common Knowledge, 10*(3), 463–484. Retrieved from Project MUSE database.

Whaanga, H. (2012). *The ethics, processes and procedures associated with the digitisation of the Pei Jones Collection.* Retrieved from http://mediacentre.maramatanga. ac.nz/content/digitisation-research-part-three-dr-h%C4%93mi-whaanga.

1 An assemblage – a collector, a collection, an indigenous community and a museum

Disassembling a heritage network – people and things, events and effects

It is now time to meet the participants in the case study described in this book: Charles Smith and his dispersed collection, Ngā Paerangi iwi the source of much of this collection, and the Pitt Rivers Museum the current custodian of this collection, who together comprise a relational assemblage of people and things. A brief analysis of the socio-political situation in the mid- to late-nineteenth century at Kaiwhāiki, the home of Ngā Paerangi on the Whanganui River, will provide a contextual framework for the historical participants, describing a culture affected by change, and where the collector, Charles Smith, fits within this. An historical indigene–settler relationship in New Zealand will be articulated within the constraints of this case study. The collector's personal collecting impetus will be positioned concurrently within the evolution of the case study museum. This is a time and space delimited study that begins in the mid-nineteenth century in New Zealand and diverges around the turn of the twentieth century following the transfer of the taonga to England and their subsequent sale to the museum. Lastly, an outline of the history of the Pitt Rivers Museum within British museum culture and the discipline of anthropology will provide a contextual framework for the later analysis of current museum policy and practice relating to indigenous collections within this social and material network.

Whanganui

Whanganui is located on the west coast of the North Island of New Zealand (see Figure 1.2); the town and region take the name of the river, which, significantly, was the main highway into the interior of the island until the early

Figure 1.1 Charles Smith (standing second from left) with Ngā Paerangi leaders including Tāmati Takarangi (at left standing), Te Oti Takarangi (central figure in korowai (cloak) holding patu (weapon)), Teretiu Whakataha (at right standing), Karehana Tahau (at left seated) and their families at Kaiwhāiki, ca. 1876–7.

Copyright Pitt Rivers Museum, University of Oxford; 1998.243.18.1.

twentieth century. For more than 700 years the people of Ngā Paerangi have continuously occupied lands on the lower Whanganui River around their present marae (settlement) at Kaiwhāiki (Young, 2007, p. 16).

By the late 1830s Christianity had been introduced to Whanganui; initially by Māori converts, then by the Church Missionary Society in the early 1840s. New Zealand's founding document, the Treaty of Waitangi, was signed in Whanganui in May 1840. A settler colony of British migrants was established at the river mouth in 1841, following the alleged New Zealand Company purchase of Whanganui land from Māori ten months earlier. Eight years of controversy and misunderstanding over the land sale followed, until 'final' resolution in 1848 by British-appointed land claims commissioner, William Spain, after which the settlement rapidly expanded.

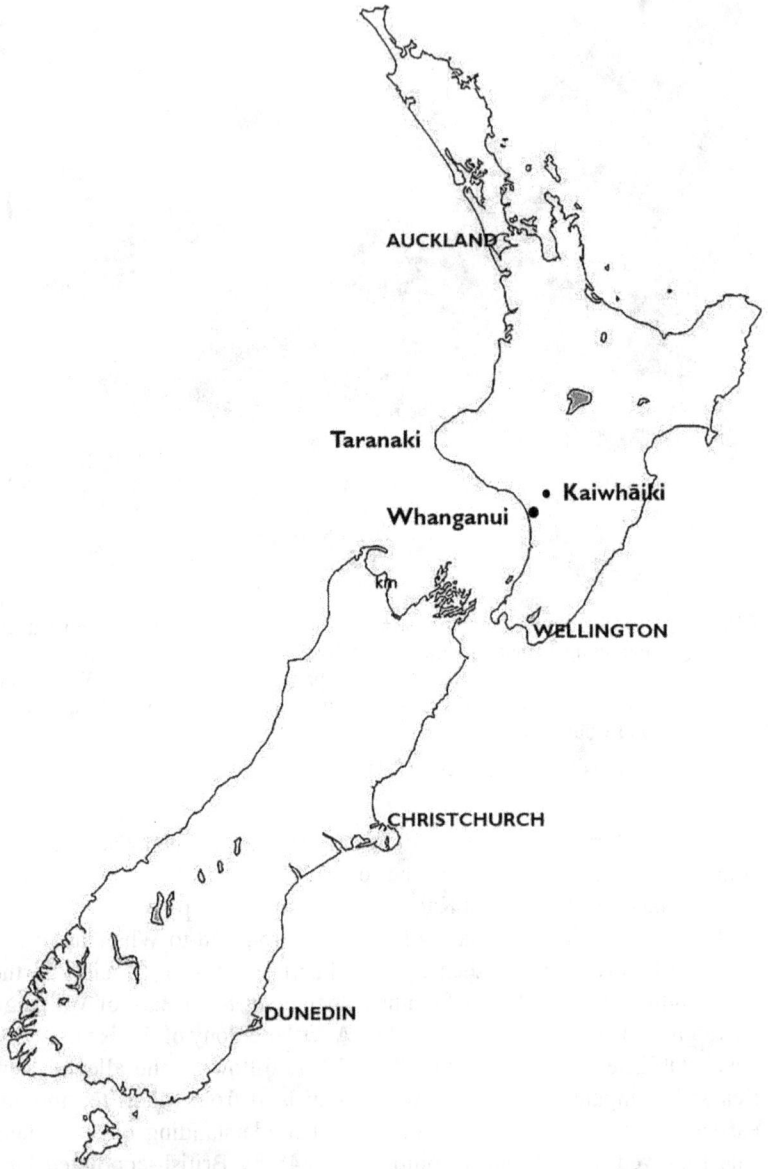

Figure 1.2 Map of New Zealand.

The indigenous community: Ngā Paerangi iwi, Whanganui

Ngā Paerangi iwi descend and take their name from Paerangi II, the great grandson of Paerangi o te Maungaroa who arrived from the ancestral homeland of Hawaiki possessing the power of flight. This eponymous ancestor has no canoe tradition (Young, 2007, p. 21). Simon, confirming this historical narrative, describes these ancestors as Kāhui Rere or 'Bird People' (ibid., p. 93). Ngā Paerangi people's descent from the ancestor Paerangi II not only establishes their relationship with other iwi, it also defines their rights to and obligations over specific lands.

Traditional Ngā Paerangi lands include some of the most extensive river flats on the Whanganui River, capable of supporting a large population in the pre-colonial period (Figure 1.3). By the mid-1800s the Kaiwhāiki area was Ngā Paerangi's main food growing area, while Tunuhaere was

Figure 1.3 Kaiwhāiki, Whanganui River.

Map data ©2018 Google, DigitalGlobe, CNES / Airbus, Horizons Regional Consortium.

a fortified pā (village) on the hill 100 metres above the Whanganui River across from Kaiwhāiki. Most Ngā Paerangi people lived at Tunuhaere until 1840, by which time a move to Kaiwhāiki had begun (White, 1851, p. 284). It has been suggested this move may have reflected Ngā Paerangi's response to the need to protect these rich Kaiwhāiki lands from the movement of up-river iwi (who wished to be closer to the advantages of European settlement) down to the lower-river (Walzl, 2004, pp. 48–49). There is also evidence that from 1844 Ngā Paerangi wished to be nearer to and have Europeans among them.

The first missionary influence at Kaiwhāiki was in 1840, when Church Missionary Society minister John Mason had a small chapel built at Tunuhaere. Reverend Richard Taylor followed three years later. Despite Taylor's efforts, however, by 1852 Kaiwhāiki had become the site of the first Catholic mission on the Whanganui River. During this period Kaiwhāiki was a "village of some 200 inhabitants" who supplied the Whanganui settlers with fruit, vegetables, flour ground at the Kaiwhāiki mill (Vibaud, n.d., p. 35) and building lumber from their timber mill established at the same time (Downes, 1921, p. 73).

Conflict between Protestant and Catholic missionaries, however, resulted in these flour mills becoming a bargaining tool for souls on the Whanganui River during this period. Considered 'a snare of Satan' by Protestant Taylor (Taylor, 1833–1873, pp. MS161/168), the Kaiwhāiki mill fell into disuse and the mission (and its millwright) moved up-river to Kauaeroa in 1854 (Vibaud, n.d., p. 19). Taylor swooped, tribal leader Te Oti Takarangi was baptised, and by 1860 Taylor had made serious inroads into Father Lampila's established Catholic congregation there (Walzl, 2004, p. 57).

During the 1860s Ngā Paerangi's upper-river cousins became involved in a new religion called Pai Mārire (good and peaceful) which combined Christian and traditional Māori beliefs and which opposed European settlement (Clark, 1975; Elsmore, 1989). It was also the religion of the Kīngitanga (Māori King Movement). Ngā Paerangi, however, maintained their alliance with the Protestant mission while supporting the Kīngitanga.

Prophetic movements had developed in New Zealand during the 1860s (Elsmore, 1989) seeking to regain Māori authority and self-determination. Pai Mārire, founded by Te Ua Haumēne, grew out of the conflict overland in Taranaki. Te Ua's statement of mana motuhake (independence) "had a profound influence on the course of Māori Christianity" (Head, 1992, p. 7). Despite the movement's ideals of goodness and peace, some followers turned to violent resistance. They were seen as rebels by Europeans and became known as Hauhau.

During this period, Ngā Paerangi were in a unique position: located amongst their lower-river cousins but, through their affiliation with the Kīngitanga (which opposed Māori land alienation), were considered 'rebels,' along with their upper-river relatives, by the settler-colonists (White, 1864–5, p. 230). Kaiwhāiki was also the assembly point for tribal groups from the south travelling overland to Taranaki (through Charles Smith's farm) in the west to support their relatives in the Taranaki wars of the 1860s (Allen, n.d.).

By 1864, however, officials would no longer accept anti-government sentiment along the lower reaches of the river. Sir Isaac Featherston, Colonial Secretary, demanded allegiance from Ngā Paerangi by threatening removal. Although Te Oti Takarangi then swore the Oath of Allegiance to the Queen, Kaiwhāiki remained a Kīngitanga village. This narrative is expanded in Chapter 3 through the effects of recent events on assemblage components which have recovered past and generated new social and material networks.

After the wars of the 1860s, Ngā Paerangi joined with lower-river people travelling to Parihaka in about 1876 to support the peaceful resistance movement of the prophets Tohu Kākahi and Te Whiti o Rongomai.[1] These religious leaders had established a community at Parihaka in Taranaki in 1866 with the blessing of Te Ua Haumēne.

During the 1870s Parihaka grew into the largest Māori settlement in the country. In response to government surveying of the confiscated southern Taranaki lands from 1878, they reclaimed land by ploughing it. As their followers were imprisoned for this, more people came to take their places. In 1881 troops ransacked Parihaka and took many people prisoner including Te Whiti and Tohu who were held without trial for two years, and a third Taranaki prophet, Tītokowaru. Te Oti Takarangi was also imprisoned.[2] Parihaka continued as a centre of non-violent resistance to settler laws until the deaths of both men in 1907 (Elsmore, 1989). Support for the cause at Parihaka had resulted for Ngā Paerangi in the sale of land to private purchasers from 1867, soon after title to Ngā Paerangi land blocks was awarded (Walzl, 2004, p. 68).

Ngā Paerangi organise themselves today around their descent from the five children of Te Rangituawaru (great-great-great-great-great-grandson of Paerangi II) and Hinekehu – Tōmairangi, Whararakia, Te Rangitokona, Te Uira and Tutamou (Rzoska, personal communication, 14 April 2013). Today Kaiwhāiki marae is home to about 50 closely related families (Simon, 2013, p. 5), and is one of two remaining Catholic marae on the Whanganui River. While the absence of material heritage for this community today is noted elsewhere, Ngā Paerangi people are renowned for whaikōrero (oratory), titonga (composition) and waiata (song).

Te Oti Takarangi (?–July 1885)

Te Oti Takarangi (see Figure 1.1) descended from Ngāti Hinekehu/Ngāti Te Uira line of Ngā Paerangi and was the leader of this tribal community during the nineteenth century. He had one son, Tāmati Te Oti, and one granddaughter, Ngārongokahira, who had no children (Rzoska, personal communication, 18 April 2013).

The few surviving contemporary accounts of Te Oti Takarangi provide a picture of a competent tribal leader in a tumultuous period of colonial history.

> Takarangi was a notable man in his way, and will be long remembered by Europeans for his unconquerable dislike to the alien race. He was a Maori of the old school and could not brook anything like opposition or dissent from his opinion on the part of the members of his tribe. When the Parihaka trouble was in full swing, he and his people who accompanied him were found to be ringleaders in every hostile movement against the whites.
>
> ("Death of Takarangi", 1885).

His obituary in the local newspaper, the *Wanganui Chronicle*, in 1885, while not altogether complimentary, also indicates that his loyalties were with his people, he was open to new alliances that advantaged his and his tribe's situation, and he was a shrewd negotiator.

Four items in the Charles Smith collection are gifts to Smith from Te Oti Takarangi: a pā kahawai (fishhook and heirloom) named Te Pā o Hinematioro, a carved tuki (wooden collar for a storage gourd), tā moko (tattoo) material, and a hei (pendant) crafted by him.

Wiremu Pātene Te Rangituawaru (?–29 December 1874)

Wiremu Pātene was the second cousin of Te Oti Takarangi and next in senior rank at Kaiwhāiki (Rzoska, personal communication, 15 April 2013). He and his wife, Taiwiri Mutumutu, had one daughter, Ngāpera Pikia also known as Te Aue. Descendants today are the Allan whānau (family group). Ngāpera Pikia gave Charles Smith a korowai (cloak). A tewhatewha (long-handled weapon) also in the Pitt Rivers Museum collection with Wiremu Pātene's name carved into the handle is likely to be a part of the Charles Smith collection as well.

Tāmati Takarangi (1852–1935)

Tāmati Takarangi, the son of Te Oti Takarangi's younger brother Ngāmako, became a leader of Ngā Paerangi after Te Oti Takarangi's death. He was renowned for his size and strength. His wife was Tīpare (Mere) Ōtene and they had two children, a son Te Rāngai Tāmati born about 1875 and a daughter Miriata Te Kahukore born about 1880 (Figure 1.4).

Figure 1.4 Tāmati Takarangi with his wife Tīpare (Mere) Ōtene and son Te Rāngai
Tāmati, ca. 1880.

Tāmati Takarangi gave Charles Smith the pākurukuru (canoe prow)
named Tunuhaere (Figure 1.5) as a memorial to his uncle Te Oti Takarangi,
and was also the source of the emblems of peace, the taiaha (weapon, ceremonial staff) named Te Maungārongo (Peacemaker) (see Figure 3.1) and
the hoeroa (long weapon, staff) named Ngā Karu o Niu Tīreni (The Eyes of
New Zealand) (see Figure 3.2 and Chapter 3).

Figure 1.5 Pākurukuru river canoe prow named Tunuhaere, 2013.
Photo by Michelle Horwood.

The contemporary actors representing Ngā Paerangi in this narrative are:

Morvin Te Anatipa Simon, rangatira (leader), kaumātua (respected elder), renowned orator, composer, kapa haka (performance) exponent, teacher and father. His personal mana (status) and support were key to Ngā Paerangi participation in this study. Despite failing health he was a guiding influence and mentor for this project. Morvin Simon died on 13 May 2014.

Hera Te Upokoira Pēina, kuia (respected elder), and, as a descendant of Takarangi-Atua, has a close affiliation with many taonga in the Charles Smith collection.

Ken Clarke, kaumātua and tribal historian, bull wrangler and Ngā Paerangi representative on Whanganui Regional Museum governing body for several years from 2001.

Haimona (Sam) Te Iki Rzoska, Ngā Paerangi whakapapa (genealogy) exponent and tribal historian, father and grandfather. Haimona Rzoska is the great great grandson of Teretiu Whakataha, Ngā Paerangi leader during the nineteenth century, and was an active participant in this project until his untimely death on 29 September 2016 at the age of 52.

Katrina Hāwira is a Māori language teacher with experience as an educator at the Museum of New Zealand Te Papa Tongarewa (Te Papa) and as a curator/kaitiaki Māori at the Whanganui Regional Museum.

These five formed the Project Team of advisors who together had the authority, cultural knowledge and expertise to represent and speak for Ngā Paerangi and provide credibility to the research. They also guided the project and assisted in the development and implementation of a project plan. For the journey to Oxford, Pēina, Rzoska and Hāwira joined:

Wīpaki Peeti, kaumātua and great grandson of Tāmati Takarangi,
Teresa Peeti, Wīpaki Peeti's daughter,
Takahia Tawaroa (Sister Makareta) and **Luana Tawaroa,** kuia and great granddaughters of Teretiu Whakataha,
Ereti (Reti) Wisneski, kuia who travelled from Australia to support her sister-in-law Hera Pēina and reconnect with her Ngā Paerangi whanaunga (relatives),
Tuata Angus, Takahia Tawaroa's niece, who travelled from New York to support her aunt in Oxford.

Ngā Paerangi are the kaitiaki (guardians) for the Charles Smith collection and have considered themselves so since research about the collection has identified the ways in which Charles Smith obtained items from their ancestors. Even though they may not be able to physically realise their guardianship nor impact on the physical or spiritual care of their taonga, they will not relinquish this responsibility.

The collector: Charles Smith, Whanganui

In 1859 Charles Smith (Figures 1.1 and 1.6) left his family and friends in England and emigrated to New Zealand. He was 26 years of age when he settled on the 2,700-acre farm, 'Te Korito' on the Whanganui River (*The Cyclopedia of New Zealand*, 1897, p. 1451) and where he lived for the next fifty years. He never married. The land comprising Charles Smith's farm had been obtained from Ngā Paerangi, was located across the Whanganui River from their settlement at Kaiwhāiki, and was adjacent to their defensive pā Tunuhaere (see Figure 1.7). Smith developed a mutually beneficial relationship with the Ngā Paerangi community obtaining from them numerous items of material culture, many of which he sent to his family in England and elsewhere (see Figure 2.7). Smith's collection, comprising

Figure 1.6 Charles Smith at his home, Te Korito, Whanganui, ca. 1880.

Copyright Pitt Rivers Museum, University of Oxford; 1998.245.198.

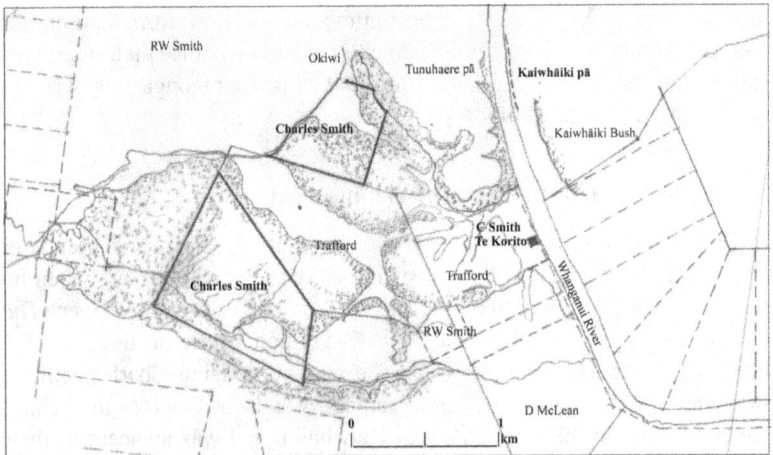

Figure 1.7 Detail of Robert Parkes' 1842 plan by C M Igglesden, 1856, showing Charles Smith's homestead, Te Korito, and farm and Kaiwhāiki pā (marae).

National Archives, Wellington, New Zealand; SO 10552 RP 440. Redrawn by John Verstappen, 2015.

around 460 indigenous heritage items, was sold to the Pitt Rivers Museum in 1923 by his nephew Alfred Collier for £50 (Balfour, n.d. (1938–1942), p. 3). More than 300 items in the Charles Smith collection had originated from New Zealand. While a number retain their biographies, revealing their immense significance within tribal narratives of the nineteenth century, many were everyday items and display the cross-fertilising of new technologies and materials with traditional Māori arts. Significantly, for Ngā Paerangi the collection represents the majority of extant taonga known to this community. This special collection is one of very few collections held in museums internationally where details of individual items, their original owners and owner communities and events associated with them have been retained alongside the items themselves.

The scene that greeted Charles Smith when he arrived in Whanganui in 1859 would have been similar to that described by fellow settler Cornelius Burnett when he arrived three years earlier. After a 183-day journey from Gravesend England, Burnett (1920, p. 16) discovered

> The mixture of military display and barbaric ascendancy, of old soldiers and old whalers, of Highland shepherds and Lowland farmers, of a sprinkling of almost all the nationalities of the world, with here and there a few English settlers, combined to make up a polyglot nondescript outlandish condition of things that took us by surprise.

With only 11 Europeans living along the river north of the town of Whanganui, Charles Smith being the farthest from town with no road extending as far as his farm, "Much of the settler's up-river traffic was performed by canoe" (Allen, n.d.).

There are few personal accounts about Charles Smith. He was a farmer employing a farm manager, William Smith; a stockman, a housekeeper,[3] as well as Martin, a 'gentleman assistant.'[4] Inferences made about his generous, inquisitive and unassuming nature from first-hand accounts that survive include that by Edith Smith, the daughter of William Smith, who described him as a "kind of fairy godfather to my family, and we had many expensive presents he gave us." He died at their home at Tauwhare in 1908 and she can remember this and that she turned six a few weeks later.[5]

Despite arriving in the colony at a tumultuous period in its fledgling history when in the Whanganui region "the fire was in the fern . . . [with] the spreading flames of war reach[ing] the up-river tribes" (Reed, 1940, p. xiv), Charles Smith developed a relationship with his Ngā Paerangi neighbours at Kaiwhāiki (see Figure 1.1). Specifically the principle chief Te Oti Takarangi, his cousin Wiremu Pātene, and his nephew Tāmati Takarangi, as well as other Māori living near or visiting Kaiwhāiki at this time including

Te Herekiekie and Takuira Tauteka of the central North Island tribe, Ngāti Tūwharetoa.

After the wars of the 1860s, George F Allen surveyed large blocks of land in the Waitōtara valley and on the Whanganui River (Kirk, 1993), including, in 1883, Charles Smith's farm. During this visit he recalls crossing the Whanganui River to Kaiwhāiki "then the abode of King Maoris," where he and his chainman were initially denied access. Returning accompanied by Smith's 'man Martin,' they attended a meeting in the whare rūnanga (council house), Te Kiritahi, where

> . . . curses against the Pakeha [European] authorities were numerous. 'Mea to Kuini!' 'Kakino te Kawanatanga!!!' 'Tama to Kawana!!!'. Martin said it was all safe, but I told him the place was all too hot for me, so he pleaded that excuse, and we made our exits as gracefully as we could. I wasn't sorry when we got over to Mr Charles Smith's side of the river.
>
> Kaiwhaiki was, in the early '60s, the assembling place of all Southern Maoris . . . all going in for many hours drill every day and finally marching northward [to Taranaki], thro Mr Smith's land, keeping inland from other Pakeha settlers.
>
> (Allen, n.d.)

This brief but graphic account illustrates the complexities of Māori-European relationships at this time on the Whanganui River. The political position of Ngā Paerangi leaders and Smith's neutrality are clearly indicated by a route to the war in Taranaki passing through his farm. Although the purpose of Allen's visit to Te Kiritahi is unclear, his anxiety is not although his role as a tool in the provincial government's process of land alienation may easily account for this. The views of Ngā Paerangi and others assembled at this meeting illustrate their support for the Kīngitanga, their dissatisfaction with, and ill feeling towards the Queen (Kuini) and her representative in New Zealand, as well as the process of governorship (kāwanatanga) as it was effected at this time.

Extant references to Te Oti Takarangi indicate the little regard in which he held the settler population. However, the nature of his relationship with Charles Smith, in general terms, can be deduced and was one of mutual respect and benefit. It is clear Smith was informally adopted into Te Oti Takarangi's extended family, becoming Te Oti Takarangi's 'Pākehā' (Salmond, 2017, p. 145). Smith was comfortable visiting the marae and interacting with Ngā Paerangi people and inviting them into his home, while other settlers, such as Allen, were less comfortable with or avoided these situations. Ngā Paerangi's overland route to Taranaki through Smith's farm remained open to them during the 1860s conflicts at a time when many out settlers were leaving the district fearful for their lives. The regard in which Smith was held by Te Oti Takarangi is clearly illustrated in a passage by G F Allen (1894, pp. 157–158),

> Sometimes when a specially rowdy party [of Māori on their way to the conflict in Taranaki] arrived, old Takarangi would go over to Mr. Charles Smith . . . and tell him he'd better go to town for a day or two and leave his keys with him. This was frequently done, and Takarangi took care that dogs, cats, and fowls were duly fed, and Mr. Smith would find everything safe on his return.

Recently, new information has come to light that expands what we know about Smith including the regard in which he was held by Ngā Paerangi. This information is from a collection of documents discovered in 2016 by Clare Fazan, a distant relative of Charles Smith. They include a note from Te Oti Takarangi who had warned Smith to go to town before the Battle of Moutoa in 1864 and was concerned as to why he had not returned.[6] A similar warning came from Wiremu Pātene in this November 1868 letter to Smith,

> Friend Greetings – You stay in town do not return for I do not know what the Hauhau are going to do – You might be taken Captive.[7]

Box 1.1   Taiaha Te Maungārongo (Peacemaker) and hoeroa Ngā Karu o Niu Tīreni (The Eyes of New Zealand)

Smith recognised the centrality of the taonga Te Maungārongo and Ngā Karu o Niu Tīreni (see Figures 3.1 & 3.2) in intertribal relationships on the Whanganui River in the nineteenth century, the former ensuring the Taranaki wars of the 1860s did not cross into the Whanganui region. For this reason he asked retired Whanganui Resident Magistrate Richard Woon to document the account of Te Korenga (Kerehoma) Tūwhāwhākia of Whanganui so a record of events could be made and the importance of these emblems of peace and authority documented.[8]

Tūwhawhakia's account provides the genealogy of Te Maungārongo from the renowned Taranaki leader Tītokowaru of Ngā Ruahine, to Whanganui leader Hōri Kīngi Te Anaua, and then to Te Anaua's nephew the formidable warrior leader Taitoko Keepa Te

Rangihiwinui who presented it to Te Oti Takarangi. Takarangi then gave it to Wiremu Pātene, 'as a peace token.' Smith added that the taiaha was "a token from Titokowaru that the war should not cross the Kaiiwi" and believed the taiaha saved his life when he was to be attacked by a Taranaki war party in February 1865. "Te Oti & Patene sent young men to Te Korito to protect friend [Smith], were three days there watching. Kereopa & war party of Tito came to Te Korito and were going to shoot [Smith] at Te Momimomi, and would have done so but for Takarangi's young men." Instead they went on to kill Taranaki settler and provincial councillor James Hewett, against the wishes of Tītokowaru.

While Ngā Karu o Niu Tīreni, the hoeroa, considered by Tūwhāwhākia "to be like a regimental flag and a thing to be saved at all regards," came from Pōtatau Te Wherowhero, the first Māori King "to [Whanganui leader] Hamarama . . . [In 1863] when it came [to Kaiwhāiki] Te Kiritahi whare was built . . . and the [Hauhau] Niu flag & pole called Potatau were erected . . ." with the hoeroa recognised as the emblem of the Kīngitanga.

Both taonga were kept by Te Oti Takarangi as "emblems of peace for some time . . ."[9] but were later 'given up' by Whanganui Māori following the taking of the Oath of Allegiance to the Crown, described by Whanganui Resident Magistrate, John White in 1865 (1864–5, pp. 116–117). Later, in 1885, they were taken by Tāmati Takarangi "to Mr Smith . . . for safekeeping." While Te Oti Takarangi did not wish these taonga to be sold, in June 1886 Tāmati Takarangi received eight pounds from Smith for them, which at the time was considered "right to give, for these weapons are important."[10]

Significantly, Smith went to great lengths to document these events which solves a puzzle that has perplexed members of Ngā Paerangi since the Charles Smith collection became known to them in 2006 – for what reason and how did such significant taonga travel the route they did, ending in Smith's possession?

These accounts and the gifts such as the fishhook Te Pā o Hinematioro presented to Charles Smith and his acknowledgement of the meaning inherent in these ritual gifting processes of reciprocity and ongoing commitment to a relationship (Henare, 2005, p. 124), as well as the willingness of Ngā Paerangi members to pass the taiaha Te Maungārongo and the hoeroa Ngā Karu o Niu Tīreni into his safekeeping, clearly establish his mana within this community. Charles Smith also hosted prominent tribal leaders in his home and others sought him out, such as Ngā Rauru leader Pehimana Manakore from Waitōtara in South Taranaki.[11]

Charles Smith took a keen interest in local affairs in Whanganui. He was involved in charitable works, contributed generously to memorial, sporting and patriotic causes, was a lieutenant in the local Militia (No. 3 (Turakina) Company) during the New Zealand wars of the 1860s (Lovegrove, 1960–9, p. 52), a member of local councils and boards, and of the Royal Colonial Institute, London and the New Zealand Institute (the Royal Society since 1933) from its inception in 1867 (*The cyclopedia of New Zealand*, 1897). He was also a friend of Whanganui museum founder and director Samuel Drew. His donation to the museum of eight volumes of the French theologian and philosopher Pluche's major work *Spectacle de la Nature* reflects a broad literary interest.

Smith brought a keen interest in exploration and collecting with him to New Zealand. In a letter to his brother-in-law in 1861 he writes at length about a six-week trek with surveyor and engineer John Rochford, traversing two to three hundred miles along the rugged West Coast of the South Island, stating, "I must say I am fond of that sort of life." He also describes their collecting efforts and, in somewhat disparaging terms, the 'insinuating way' in which Julius von Haast, explorer, geologist and founder of Christchurch's Canterbury Museum, convinces them to hand over their fauna and flora finds.[12]

His friendship with Samuel Drew however was mutually beneficial. Drew was a prolific collector of natural history specimens and items of ethnography and established a private museum in his business premises which was open to the public from 1885. He sold his collection to the city as the foundation for a public museum in 1892 (Figure 1.8). Smith became a regular donor to the Whanganui museum from 1892 (Whanganui Regional Museum Collection Register 1892–1923) and accompanied Drew on a number of specimen collecting trips around New Zealand and to the East Coast of Australia (Drew, 1896, p. 288). These trips included one to the Bay of Islands in 1898 returning with 3,352 fish specimens and the nationally significant missionary Williams' family barrel organ (*Wanganui Chronicle* July 23, 1898).

Richard Taylor, Church Missionary Society missionary to Whanganui, may also have influenced Charles Smith's interests. Taylor was a keen observer of Māori language and customary practices, a naturalist with interests in linguistics, ethnology, botany, zoology and geology, and a collector. His interests are evident today in a number of published books including *Te Ika a Maui* (1855) and *The Past and Present of New Zealand* (1868) as well as his journals, manuscripts and sketch books, a plant named in his honour,

Figure 1.8 Wanganui Public Museum, 1898.

Photographer A D Willis. Copyright Whanganui Regional Museum, Whanganui; 1802.3375.

Dactylanthus taylorii, and an important collection of ethnographic items in the Whanganui Regional Museum collection. In his journal he recorded that he dined at Charles Smith's home on a couple of occasions in 1866.[13]

The Great Exhibition in London in 1851 was pivotal in inspiring anthropological thought of amateur scholars of Smith's generation (Chapman, 1985; Harris, 2012). He lived in London during this period (it is likely that he was still a student at University College School), so it can also be surmised that this Exhibition, with its displays of British expansion and empire, exposed him to the potential opportunities which emigration to the colonies might afford.

There is no evidence, however, that Charles Smith was influenced by anthropological scholarship during the mid- to late-nineteenth century, nor by Darwin's seminal work published in 1857. Although it would be tempting to conclude that he was a member of the emerging Victorian anthropological elite who had met Pitt Rivers at meetings of the Ethnological Society of London, this seems unlikely. He was neither a member of nor a contributor to learned society publications of the period, such as the Ethnological

Society of London or the Royal Anthropological Institute (Walpole, personal communication, 24 June 2015), but rather seemed to have focussed his attention when in London on the Royal Colonial Institute. His membership of the Institute at some point following its foundation in 1868 provided influences that reinforced his collecting pursuits.

The museum: Pitt Rivers Museum, Oxford

Europeans have knowledge, and the rest of the world has objects?

Walter Mignolo[14]

The social and material network that is the Pitt Rivers Museum is the final constituent of the research assemblage to be considered here. This museum (Figure 1.9) was founded in 1884 when Lieutenant-General Augustus Henry Lane Fox Pitt Rivers donated a collection of around 20,000 objects to the University of Oxford. While, as Harrison (2013, p. 8) notes, the "rise of ethnographic collecting in Western Europe was closely associated with the projects of colonialism . . . and imperialism . . . and the development of

Figure 1.9 Oxford University Museum of Natural History and Pitt Rivers Museum, Oxford, 2013.

Photo by Michelle Horwood.

the professional field of anthropology," Chapman (1985, p. 43) asserts, Pitt Rivers' donation "placed anthropology in Britain for the first time within an academic setting" and went on to shape anthropology as a discipline at Oxford.

Establishment of Pitt Rivers' collection at the University Museum founded a new Ethnographic Department, with Pitt Rivers' focus on his collection organised by typologies, as was then the recognised classification system for natural specimens. He prioritised "form and function over cultural origin and age" (Larson, 2008, p. 91) to present an 'evolution' of human ideas, arguing that culture should be understood as nature was. Appointment of a lecturer in anthropology in 1884 established this academic field at Oxford University. With the focus on objects in museums rather than concerns with social relations and fieldwork, however, Oxford anthropology lagged behind anthropological thought elsewhere until the late 1960s (ibid., p. 97, Conn, 1998). Most literature however focuses upon an analysis of Pitt Rivers' classification system without reference to the way in which objects are displayed today, which instead emphasises cross-cultural comparisons of technologies (Figure 1.10). As staff assert, displays are a celebration of the

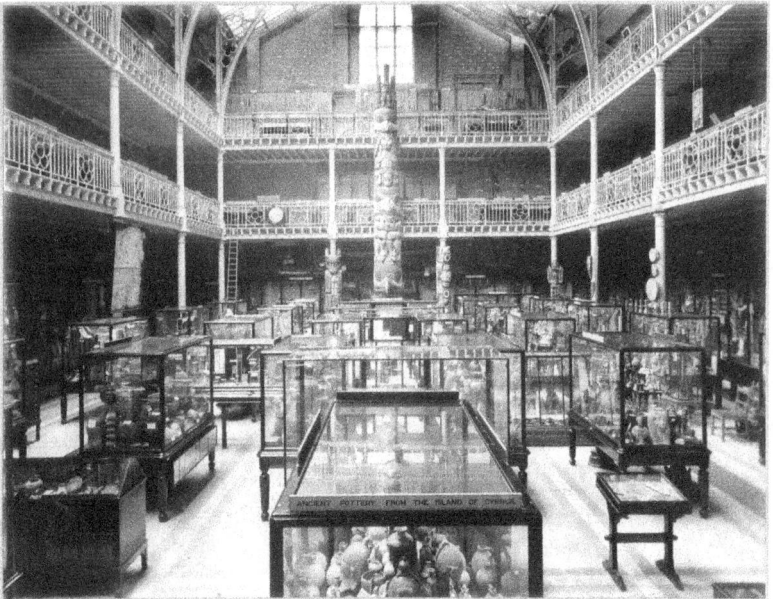

Figure 1.10 Pitt Rivers Museum, c.1901.

Copyright Pitt Rivers Museum, University of Oxford; 1998.267.269.3.

creativity of the peoples of the world (Coote, personal communication, 15 November 2013).

By World War II museum anthropology was, Stocking (1985, p. 9) proposes, "stranded in an institutional, methodological, and theoretical backwater" with anthropology moving into the university and the abandonment of object based study (Conn, 1998; Henare, 2005). Field ethnographers no longer collected objects with museum acquisitions obtained instead from untrained people. Collections also became increasingly inaccessible to researchers and care was often inadequate (Stocking, 1985, p. 9).

But then things changed dramatically. There was an evolution in exhibition practice from the 1960s with a push towards professional accreditation (as described by Nancy Lurie 1981, cited by Stocking, 1985, p. 10). Since the late 1960s indigenous communities "have come forward as actors in the world of museum anthropology" (ibid., p. 11) with the decolonisation of museum practice providing new challenges (Barringer & Flynn, 1998; Clifford, 1997, 2004; Karp & Lavine, 1991). New Zealand responded with *Te Maori* (Mead, 1986).[15] This, however, has not been easy for the Pitt Rivers Museum to realise. As Coote states, "the difficulty in the Pitt Rivers is to find the space to, in a meaningful way, [provide] an insight into one particular or any number of world views" (personal communication, 15 November 2013).

Since the 1980s, "the material turn in anthropology has been particularly influential" through recognising that objects (like persons) have agency (Harris & O'Hanlon, 2013, p. 8) and a role in social relationships (Hicks, 2010, p. 64). Authority over ownership and management of objects in Western museum collections has also been questioned through, what Stocking (1985, p. 11) describes as the "emergence of new national consciousness . . . [and] heightened domestic radicalism." A new museology arose in the second half of the twentieth century in response to a perceived need for the role of museums in society to change (McCall & Gray, 2013; Vergo, 1989). Stephen Weil aptly describes this in 1999 in the title of his article "From Being about Something to Being for Somebody." A second wave of this new museology (Boast, 2011, p. 59) has followed, which is having an impact with regard to the meaning of museum objects to their communities of origin and the role of museums in shaping community identity and assisting community development through engagement and shared management of heritage items.

Since 1884, donations to the Pitt Rivers Museum have resulted in a collection today of around "300,000 objects, a similar number of historical photographs, plus sound recordings, manuscripts and library" (Coote, personal communication, 15 November 2013). The current thematic display method is a distinct feature of this museum. It retains the original organisation of the displays, although it is no longer influenced by Pitt Rivers' ideas about the evolution of design; rather, as stated above, it celebrates creativity and innovation.

Pitt Rivers Museum today

Ethnology museums are, as Kirshenblatt-Gimblett (2012, p. 198) states, "agents of deculturation, as the final resting place for evidence of the success of missionizing and colonizing efforts, among others, that preserve (in the museum) what was wiped out (in the community)." They have thus been self-perpetuating through reinventing their relevance to contemporary society in the context of the disappearance of culture through collecting, and its subsequent salvage through ethnology (ibid., p. 199). Ethnographic collecting has therefore created a fragmentary assemblage of objects (Kirshenblatt-Gimblett, 1998), separated from or devoid of their intangible qualities, further enabling the self-perpetuation of ethnographic study through their recontextualisation. Strategies to identify the 'missing fragments' are having some success (Byrne, 2013; Satterthwait, 2008; Torrence & Clarke, 2013).

The current resurgence of interest in material culture studies is also valid here (Hicks & Beaudry, 2010; Knappett, 2005; Thomas, Adams, Lythberg, Nuku, & Salmond, 2016; Tilley, Keane, Kuchler, Rowlands, & Spyer, 2006), particularly as a means to reconcile understanding of the object as both event and effect. Of relevance is Hicks' (2010, p. 94) suggestion that attention to practice (he states 'field practice' in relation to both archaeology and anthropology, from which I infer museum practice as well) rather than just theory "could allow new kinds of cross-disciplinary work in 'material-culture' studies to develop." Krmpotich and Peers (2013) emphasise this in the detailed documentation of their collaborative project with Haida people, and point out that such detailed studies of current practice are under-represented in the literature. Addressing this gap in the literature is a central aim of this book, achieved in particular through the emergence of new events and effects resulting from interactions between the network entities of Ngā Paerangi, the Charles Smith collection and the Pitt Rivers Museum.

Hicks' (2010) concise history of the 'material-cultural' turn within the disciplines of anthropology and archaeology provides a clear framework for understanding the nature of Charles Smith's collecting activities, which occurred during a period when the West was attempting to categorise world cultures across time and space. Public museums were instrumental in this process. They provided the collections, enthusiasm and expertise whereby material representations of culture could be assessed, and placed within the schema of cultural evolution and interrelatedness, which at the Pitt Rivers

Museum had expanded from the collecting of antiquities to embrace Pitt Rivers' evolutionary and typological organisational principles.

In recent decades at the Pitt Rivers Museum, consideration of issues relating to rightful ownership or circumstances of acquisition, control of representation of meaning, and 'appropriate' care over the items in its collection have contributed to developments in museology and innovations in curatorial praxis in a number of ways. As Harris and O'Hanlon (2013, p. 10) have stated, "Behind the scenes in many ethnographic museums, a postcolonial intellectual refurbishment has in fact often already been conducted, even if it may not be fully apparent to the public." Through exhibitions, staff have produced thematic displays of topical issues, or explored issues of cultural identity. But the most significant advancements for indigenous communities have been those resulting from successful significant funding bids providing online access to collection information, as well as those that have engaged directly with these communities, such as The Tibet Album (Harris, 2012) and the Blackfoot Shirts Project (Brown, Peers, & Richardson, 2012). The literature on this work is expanding (Brown & Peers, 2015; Krmpotich, Peers, with the Haida Repatriation Committee, & staff of the Pitt Rivers Museum and British Museum, 2013; Morton & Oteyo, 2015; Peers, 2013).

Harris and O'Hanlon (2013) describe engagement with indigenous communities and addressing colonial legacies of acquisition as only two of the issues, suggesting that experience may have disinclined curators to undertake activities "that recall the involvement of museums with the colonial project" (ibid., p. 10). Although others suggest a more radical trust is required for genuinely collaborative projects which "may help museums to become more aware of their legacies of prejudice" to thus become spaces for democratic exchange (Lynch & Alberti, 2010, p. 30). This would enable museums to respond effectively to their often diverse constituencies to maintain relevance today. Reconciling this with the need to fulfil the often political agendas and requirements of their funders can, however, be challenging (Harris & O'Hanlon, 2013, p. 11). Harris and O'Hanlon (ibid., p. 12) conclude that the internet and thus the 'digitally distributed museum' may be the ethnographic museum's saviour in addressing the limitations of their physical manifestation in a globalised and multicultural world.

During a month-long visit to Oxford in 2013, I was able to observe, firsthand, current museum practice at the Pitt Rivers Museum in relation to collection access for indigenous originating communities. One outcome of the cumulative experience of research visits by indigenous communities has been the development of institutional procedures to ensure staff respond appropriately to indigenous visitors to the collections, with detailed itineraries developed to incorporate appropriate hosting. Staff are exemplary in their customer service focus, endeavouring to ensure visitors to the collection are satisfied with visit outcomes. The staff believe that indigenous communities received special attention, as Peers states, "I know that we bend over backwards to provide every kind of access desired by individuals with particular genealogical connections to objects" (personal communication, 12 November 2013).

Peers, as one of the leading scholar-practitioners in this field of museum–indigenous community relationships, after arriving from Canada in 1998 set about establishing new procedures and protocols for responding to these communities, which have been built on subsequently. As she maintains,

> I learned not to present myself as the scholarly authority. I learned that I had . . . one set of perspectives, and that there were others . . . I was prepared to foreground indigenous community needs and agendas and not see collections-based research as a kind of data gathering exercise to benefit the museum.
>
> (ibid.)

Peers shares these experiences and skills within the institution and this action implements changes not only in museum practice but also in the philosophical underpinnings of display and interpretation. During 2013 Pacific curator Jeremy Coote (personal communication, 6 November 2013) was redeveloping displays centred upon material collected on the voyages of Captain Cook and thinking about "linking objects to communities, to people and events" rather than just focussing upon the objects themselves. This is a paradigmatic shift in the contextualisation of this material, where emphasis until now has been placed on unpacking the post-collecting history by anthropologically trained research staff. To foreground the cultural origins of items that are more usually linked to Cook's voyages and as testimony to collecting practices, is a significant development for the Pacific Collections at this institution.

Although it is undeniable the Pitt Rivers Museum does indeed 'bend over backwards' to accommodate research visits from indigenous communities, and they are constrained in their responses to requests for access by available resources, little has been published that expands on the experiences they have the privilege of being a part of in their various roles at the institution. There are notable exceptions (Brown et al., 2012; Krmpotich & Peers, 2011; Krmpotich et al., 2013; Peers & Brown, 2009). The staff are recognised for the range of publications they produce on different museum collections with theoretical and broader museological content. More detailed accounts, however, describing the complex processes involved in connecting communities and collections, also the special opportunities that produce new knowledge or articulate privileged cultural knowledge that they are exposed to would progress this field significantly, as Peers has achieved for North American communities (Krmpotich & Peers, 2013; Peers, 2013). Pitt Rivers is not, however, the only museum to fail in this regard.

Conclusion

In this chapter I have described the three constituent parts of a research assemblage that I will use subsequently as a framework in the analysis of the historical and contemporary relationships between them. One constituent, Ngā Paerangi, recognise that their uninterrupted occupation of lands around Kaiwhāiki has given them strength and unity as a people and that their strategic location along the Whanganui River provided advantages during the nineteenth century, including proximity to the fledgling Whanganui settler colony at the river mouth. At that time a mutually beneficial relationship was developed with another constituent in this assemblage, their 'Pākehā,' the farmer Charles Smith who was a neighbour living within their tribal boundaries. Smith was comfortable within the settler community but was equally so with his Māori neighbours. This is reflected by the items he received from Māori leaders and his acknowledgement of the meaning inherent in the associated ritual gifting processes of reciprocity and ongoing commitment to a relationship expressed through his hospitality towards and descriptions to family of his Māori friends to family. With the transference of these gifts to family in England and subsequently to the third assemblage constituent, the Pitt Rivers Museum, the kaitiakitanga (guardianship) responsibilities of Ngā Paerangi over these have re-emerged in the reassembling of these constituents in the present. At the same time the social and material network that is a university museum in Oxford, where evidence of the results of the relationship between ethnographic collecting and colonisation are clearly visible, is repositioning itself today to re-engage with descendant communities.

Notes

1 Extract from Māori Land Court Minutes referred to in evidence of Kerehoma Tūwhāwhākia, 9 December 1897, Whanganui Minute Book, volume 139.
2 Letter Te Oti Takarangi to Charles Smith, 1 February 1882, Whanganui Regional Museum Collection 2017.34.1 Charles Smith Papers; MS304–1–26.
3 Letter Susan Collier to her children, 2 December 1886, Whanganui Regional Museum Collection 2017.34.1 Charles Smith Papers; MS304–1–32, page 4.
4 Letter Charles Smith in Whanganui to his mother in England, 29 December 1861, Whanganui Regional Museum Collection 2017.34.1 Charles Smith Papers; MS304–1–17.
5 Letter Edith Smith to Brian Henderson, 18 November 1985, Whanganui Regional Museum Collection 1985.62.

6 Letter Wiremu Pātene to Charles Smith, 14 May 1864, Whanganui Regional Museum Collection, 2017.34.1 Charles Smith Papers; MS304–1–13
7 Translation of a letter Wiremu Pātene to Charles Smith, 14 November 1868, Whanganui Regional Museum Collection, 2017.34.1 Charles Smith Papers; MS304–1–17.
8 Letter Charles Smith to Richard Woon, January 18, 1886, Whanganui Regional Museum Collection 2017.34.1 Charles Smith Papers; MS304–1–28.
9 Translation of letter Tāmati Takarangi to Charles Smith, June 2, 1886, Whanganui Regional Museum Collection 2017.34.1 Charles Smith Papers; MS304–1–30.
10 Ibid.
11 Pitt Rivers Museum. (1923). *Charles Smith Collection Related Documents File.* Oxford: Pitt Rivers Museum.
12 Letter Charles Smith to Tom Smith, 2 March 1861, Whanganui Regional Museum Collection 2017.34.1 Charles Smith Papers; MS304–1–2.
13 Richard Taylor Journal, 23 & 27 November 1866, transcript, Whanganui Regional Museum Collection 2000.4.168; MS161/13 Jun 1865 – Sep 1868.
14 A provocative question from renowned semiotician and literary theorist Walter Mignolo to initiate a conversation with Jette Sandahl, director Museum of Copenhagen, during 'The Future of Ethnographic Museums: A Public Conversation', Critical Curatorship Workshop, Critical Heritage Studies, University of Gothenburg, Gothenburg, 22 May 2013.
15 In New Zealand, involvement of Māori communities in museums has generally been described within the temporal framework of *Te Maori*, an exhibition that toured the United States and New Zealand from 1984 to 1987, after which there was a major realignment of museum processes, resulting in indigenous advocacy and self-determinism.

References

Allen, G. F. (1894). *Willis's guide book of new route for tourists: Auckland – Wellington, via the hot springs, Taupo, the volcanoes, and the Wanganui River.* Wanganui: A D Willis.

Allen, G. F. (n.d.). *George Frederic Allen's reminiscences.* (1959.79). Whanganui: Whanganui Regional Museum.

Balfour, H. (n.d. (1938–1942)). *Collections VIII: Ramsden, Roscoe, Sarawak, Smith, Talbot, Thomas, Tylor, Walker* (Vol. VIII). Oxford: Pitt Rivers Museum.

Barringer, T. J., & Flynn, T. (Eds.). (1998). *Colonialism and the object: Empire, material culture and the museum.* London: Routledge.

Boast, R. (2011). Neocolonial collaboration: Museum as contact zone revisited. *Museum Anthropology, 34*(1), 56–70.

Brown, A. K., & Peers, L. (2015). The Blackfoot Shirts Project: "Our ancestors have come to visit". In S. Macdonald & H. R. Leahy (Eds.), *The international handbooks of museum studies: Museum transformations* (Vol. 4, pp. 263–288). Oxford: Wiley-Blackwell.

Brown, A. K., Peers, L. L., & Richardson, H. (2012). *Kaahsinnooniksi Ao'toksisawooyawa. Our ancestors have come to visit: Reconnections with historic blackfoot shirts.* Oxford: Pitt Rivers Museum.

Burnett, C. (1920). Wanganui in 1856: First impressions and observations of a new arrival. In J. P. Belcher (Ed.), *Wanganui from 1856 to 1929* (pp. 15–30). Wanganui: Evans, Cobb & Sharpe.

Byrne, S. (2013). Exposing the "heart" of the museum: The archaeological sensibility in the storeroom. In R. Harrison, S. Byrne, & A. Clarke (Eds.), *Reassembling the collection: Indigenous agency and ethnographic collections* (pp. 199–228). New Mexico: School for Advanced Research (SAR) Press.

Chapman, W. R. (1985). Arranging ethnology: A.H.L.F. Pitt Rivers and the typological tradition. In G. Stocking (Ed.), *Objects and others: Essays on museums and material culture* (Vol. 3, pp. 15–48). Madison, WI: The University of Wisconsin Press.

Clark, P. (1975). *"Hauhau": The Pai Mārire search for Māori identity*. Auckland: Auckland University Press.

Clifford, J. (1997). *Routes: Travel and translation in the late twentieth century*. Cambridge, MA: Harvard University Press.

Clifford, J. (2004). Looking several ways: Anthropology and native heritage in Alaska. *Current Anthropology, 45*(1), 5–30.

Conn, S. (1998). *Museums and American intellectual life, 1876–1926*. Chicago: University of Chicago Press.

The cyclopedia of New Zealand. (1897). (Vol. 1). Wellington: Cyclopedia Co.

Death of Takarangi, the Kaiwhaike chief. (1885, August 3). *Wanganui Chronicle*, p. 2.

Downes, T. W. (1921). *History of and guide to the Wanganui river*. Wanganui: Wanganui Herald Newspaper Company Limited.

Drew, S. H. (1896). On formol for preservation of natural history specimens. *Transactions and Proceedings of the Royal Society of New Zealand, 29*, 288–290.

Elsmore, B. (1989). *Mana from heaven: A century of Maori prophets in New Zealand*. New Zealand: Moana Press.

Harris, C. (2012). *The museum on the roof of the world: Art, politics and the representation of Tibet*. Chicago: University of Chicago Press.

Harris, C., & O'Hanlon, M. (2013). The future of the enthnographic museum. *Anthropology Today, 29*(1), 8–12.

Harrison, R. (2013). Reassembling ethnographic museum collections. In R. Harrison, S. Byrne, & A. Clarke (Eds.), *Reassembling the collection: Indigenous agency and ethnographic collections* (pp. 3–35). New Mexico: School for Advanced Research (SAR) Press.

Head, L. (1992). The gospel of Te Ua Haumene. *The Journal of the Polynesian Society, 101*(1), 7–44.

Henare, A. (2005). *Museums, anthropology and imperial exchange*. New York: Cambridge University Press.

Hicks, D. (2010). The material-cultural turn: Event and effect. In D. Hicks & M. C. Beaudry (Eds.), *The Oxford handbook of material culture studies* (pp. 25–98). Oxford: Oxford University Press.

Hicks, D., & Beaudry, M. C. (Eds.). (2010). *The Oxford handbook of material culture studies*. Oxford: Oxford University Press.

Karp, I., & Lavine, S. (1991). *Exhibiting cultures: The poetics and politics of museum display*. Washington: Smithsonian Institution Press.

Kirk, A. (1993). Allen, George Frederic *Dictionary of New Zealand biography. Te ara – the encyclopedia of New Zealand*. Wellington: Manatū Taonga Ministry for Culture and Heritage.

Kirshenblatt-Gimblett, B. (1998). *Destination culture: Tourism, museums, and heritage*. Berkeley: University of California Press.

Kirshenblatt-Gimblett, B. (2012). From ethnology to heritage: The role of the museum. In B. Kirshenblatt-Gimblett (Ed.), *Museum studies: An anthology of contexts* (pp. 195–201). Chichester, West Sussex: Wiley-Blackwell.

Knappett, C. (2005). *Thinking through material culture: An interdisciplinary perspective*. Philadelphia: University of Pennsylvania Press.

Krmpotich, C., & Peers, L. L. (2011). The scholar-practitioner expanded: An indigenous and museum research network. *Museum Management and Curatorship, 26*(5), 421–440.

Krmpotich, C., Peers, L. L., Haida Repatriation Committee, & staff of the Pitt Rivers Museum and British Museum. (2013). *This is our life: Haida material heritage and changing museum practice*. Vancouver: University of British Columbia Press.

Larson, F. (2008). Anthropological landscaping: General Pitt Rivers, the Ashmolean, the University Museum and the shaping of an Oxford discipline. *Journal of the History of Collections, 20*(1), 85–100.

Lovegrove, C. L. (1960–9). *Military records of the Wanganui-Rangitikei districts, 1860–1900*. Whanganui: Wanganui Founders Society.

Lurie, N. (1981). Museumland revisited. *Human Organization, 40*(2), 180–187.

Lynch, B. T., & Alberti, S. J. M. M. (2010). Legacies of prejudice: Racism, co-production and radical trust in the museum. *Museum Management and Curatorship, 25*(1), 13–35.

McCall, V., & Gray, C. (2013). Museums and the "new museology": Theory, practice and organisational change. *Museum Management and Curatorship, 29*(1), 19–35.

Mead, S. M. (1986). *Magnificent Te Maori = Te Maori whakahirahira: He korero whakanui i Te Maori*. Auckland: Heinemann.

Morton, C., & Oteyo, G. (2015). The Paro Manene Project: Exhibiting and researching photographic histories in Western Kenya. In S. Macdonald & H. R. Leahy (Eds.), *The international handbooks of museum studies: Museum transformations* (Vol. 4, pp. 311–336). Oxford: Wiley-Blackwell.

Peers, L. L. (2013). "Ceremonies of renewal": Visits, relationships, and healing in the museum space. *Museum Worlds: Advances in Research, 1*(1), 136–152.

Peers, L. L., & Brown, A. K. (2009). Colonial photographs and postcolonial relationships: The Kainai-Oxford photographic histories project. In A. M. Timpson (Ed.), *First nations, first thoughts: The impact of indigenous thought in Canada* (pp. 123–144). Vancouver: University of British Columbia Press.

Reed, A. H. (1940). John White: A biographical sketch. In J. White (Ed.), *Revenge: A love tale of the Mount Eden tribe*. Wellington: Reed Publishing (NZ) Ltd.

Salmond, A. (2017). *Tears of Rangi: Experiments across worlds*. Auckland: Auckland University Press.

Satterthwait, L. (2008). Collection as artefacts: The making and thinking of anthropological museum collections. In N. Peterson, L. Allen, & L. Hamby (Eds.), *The makers and making of indigenous Australian museum collections* (pp. 29–60). Melbourne: Melbourne University Press.

Simon, M. T. (2013). *Taku whare e. Kaiwhāiki Marae. Me ōku mahara* (Vol. III). Whanganui: Mōku Whānau Trust.

Stocking, G. (1985). Essays on museums and material culture. In G. Stocking (Ed.), *Objects and others: Essays on museums and material culture* (Vol. 3). Madison, WI: University of Wisconsin Press.

Taylor, R. (1833–1873). *Journal*. (2000.4.168). Whanganui: Whanganui Regional Museum.

Thomas, N., Adams, J., Lythberg, B., Nuku, M., & Salmond, A. (Eds.). (2016). *Artefacts of encounter: Cook's voyages, colonial collecting and museum histories*. Dunedin: Otago University Press.

Tilley, C. Y., Keane, W., Kuchler, S., Rowlands, M., & Spyer, P. (2006). *Handbook of material culture*. London: Sage Publications.

Torrence, R., & Clarke, A. (2013). Creative colonialism: Locating indigenous strategies in ethnographic museum collections. In R. Harrison, S. Byrne, & A. Clarke (Eds.), *Reassembling the collection: Indigenous agency and ethnographic collections* (pp. 171–195). New Mexico: School for Advanced Research (SAR) Press.

Vergo, P. (1989). *The new museology*. London: Reaktion Books.

Vibaud, F. J. M. (n.d.). *The Pezant Lampila regime 1850–1860*. Wellington: The Society of Mary in the Wanganui Taranaki District. Society of Mary Archives.

Walzl, T. (2004). *Whanganui Southern Cluster: Overview of land issues research report*. Whanganui: Southern Whanganui Claimant Cluster.

White, J. (1851). *Resident Magistrate's outward letterbook*. (New Munster 8 45//175–450). Wellington: Archives New Zealand.

White, J. (1864–5). *Resident Magistrate's court outward letterbook*. (R19791205, JC Wanganui 1 5/5 1864–5). Wellington: Archives New Zealand.

Young, D. (2007). *Southern Whanganui Cluster WAI903 traditional history report*. Wellington: Crown Forestry Rental Trust.

2 Museum encounters – Ngā Paerangi travel to Oxford

Literature exploring the ways in which museums are seeking to engage with indigenous originating communities and the need to move beyond the asymmetry of the contact zone model through shared authority is increasing, as stated previously. Onciul's 'engagement zone,' for example, is "a complex and unpredictable space" (Onciul, 2013, p. 78) where the perspectives of community participants and the importance of inter-community collaboration are emphasised. These have the potential to begin the task of decolonising the museum as "participants continually negotiate the rules of exchange, challenging and debating power and authority" (ibid., pp. 84–5). As I have also identified, the challenges of geographical distance for museums and indigenous communities for forging relationships are often used as opportunities for development; such as the *Inuvialuit Smithsonian Project* (Lyons, Hennessy, Arnold, & Joe, 2011), which has many parallels to the present project, and the Great Lakes Research Alliance which promotes innovative collaborative practices (de Stecher & Loyer, 2009). Awareness by indigenous communities of their material heritage held in museum collections has increased in recent decades, as a result of online collection databases and the development of digital platforms and databases to return cultural information and objects to communities (Horwood, 2017).

In the previous chapter, the components of an assemblage were described, as well as contextual information that helped position these components, so as to consider contemporary relationships between them today. In this chapter, the effects of face-to-face encounters on this contemporary relationship development between an indigenous community and a museum, framed around a collection of indigenous material heritage, are discussed. Analysis of qualitative data from interviews with museum staff and members of the originating community, as well as participant observation, contribute to this. Together, this reveals information about the reasons Ngā Paerangi people were unaware of the existence of this group of taonga until recently, as well as their viewpoint on the sale of this collection to a museum, the museum's location 19,000 km distant, and their ability to access and care for these taonga. The Pitt Rivers Museum's growing awareness of a responsibility to work with indigenous communities to help them care for, document and interpret their ancestral heritage will be revealed, as well as the benefits they gain from engaging with originating communities.

Iwi encounters: Whanganui, New Zealand

> To reconnect with those taonga is to reconnect with the people.
>
> Morvin Simon[1]

This research contributes to the literature that is re-evaluating the way in which museums and indigenous communities interact, and the methods by which a reframing of ontologies progresses museological responsibilities in the early twenty-first century (as described by authors such as Allen & Hamby, 2011; Bolton, Thomas, Bonshek, Adams, & Burt, 2013; Krmpotich, Peers, with the Haida Repatriation Committee, & staff of the Pitt Rivers Museum and British Museum, 2013). To recap, in 2006 a reconnection was made between Ngā Paerangi iwi and a collection of their taonga at the Pitt Rivers Museum. In 2013, a group of Ngā Paerangi people travelled to England and became reacquainted with these taonga on behalf of their iwi. The museum also had its first opportunity to host a tribal Māori group and participate in their reconnection experience.

A strategy for interaction

A hui-ā-iwi (tribal meeting) in 2012 gauged support for this project. Participants in this hui raised issues of ownership and repatriation, a not unexpected response given the observation that few were aware until this time of the existence of so many singularly important Ngā Paerangi taonga. At the conclusion of this hui, approval to proceed was unanimous and the project's primary aim, to develop a relationship with the museum initiated by Ngā Paerangi, was confirmed. The overarching focus of the project was identified as one of reconnection not repatriation through a spiritual journey to Oxford to undertake appropriate and necessary customary practices to safeguard the taonga, the museum staff and themselves.

Research and planning commenced. Over the next 15 months potential cultural and social outcomes of the project were identified, funding was sought, a Protocol Agreement between iwi and museum was developed identifying objectives and desired outcomes, interviews with key stakeholders were completed, and regular Project Team and wider stakeholder meetings were held.

Observations from an outsider

Due to the numerous commitments and the number of people available with the time, resources and skills required, Ngā Paerangi were not able to respond as effectively to this opportunity as they might have been, given more time for planning and discussion.[2] Instead, the responsibility for moving forward rested on the shoulders of a small group. At this time, Ngā Paerangi members were involved in the Waitangi Tribunal Whanganui River Claim (WAI167), and tribal leader, Simon, as mentioned, suffered from chronic ill health.

From a Pākehā (New Zealander of European descent) observer's perspective, new situations arose where participants initially were indecisive and therefore anxious about appropriate actions. Concurring with Onciul (2013, p. 79), there are "potential risks, costs, and benefits for participants who enter into the complex and unpredictable space of engagement zones." For Ngā Paerangi participants, several significant issues arose.

The welcome and introductions to staff on first arrival at the Pitt Rivers Museum did not fulfil a number of Māori customary requirements for the wellbeing of both the Ngā Paerangi group and museum staff. With no ceremonial welcome, the usual opportunity to greet each other, acknowledge the living and the dead, and refer to the reason for the visit, were not possible, creating confusion and unease. However, as Atkinson (2014, p. 78, citing Patterson, 1992) describes, the set of values and beliefs embodied within tikanga Māori (customary protocols) that guide behaviour are "able to adapt to changing circumstances" and did so on this occasion (although with some trepidation). Members of the group were asked to introduce themselves and describe what they saw as outcomes of the visit to Oxford. One member of the group described this uncomfortable experience using the proverb "Kāore te kūmara e kōrero mō tōna māngaro." (The sweet potato does not say how sweet it is.[3])

The gifts presented at the farewell ceremony, although considered an appropriate exchange for the 'gifts' they had received through the manaaki (care) of staff and the encounter with taonga, expanded from key staff to all staff members the group had met. This created considerable stress and was a significant strain on the groups' resources.

Rzoska had indicated he wished to take water from the Whanganui River with him to use at the museum. Water is an important aspect of tikanga to do with cleansing, clearing or neutralising the tapu or sacredness of a situation or thing. Other ceremonies would involve specific chants and prayers. Ngā

Paerangi effected the majority of these processes at the museum, although I did not observe any use of water beyond that by individuals for their own personal safety. Rzoska, in particular, may have felt uncomfortable and therefore unwilling to enact aspects of tikanga which would appear out of place in this environment.

I do acknowledge that this is my perspective and the Ngā Paerangi participants did not dwell upon aspects they had no control over. Instead, they focused upon the positive outcomes. As Hāwira stated in retrospect, the group were not "fazed by not knowing what they would be encountering, that was the Māori way, they just went for it" (personal communication, 13 July 2014). All group members appeared very happy with their individual experiences in Oxford and excited to share these experiences with whānau.

Museum encounters: Oxford, England

Over the past 25 years, there has been a shift in the primary focus of the museum from being *about* things to being *for* people, with increased attention turning to social responsiveness and intangible heritage. Redefining curatorship as social practice, Kreps (2003, pp. 320–321) argues,

Figure 2.1 Teresa Peeti with her ancestor Te Oti Takarangi's taiaha, Pitt Rivers Museum, 2013.

Photo by Michelle Horwood.

"acknowledges the interplay among objects, people, and society," enabling "more holistic, integrated and culturally relative approaches to curating" and the reassembling of objects and people. This can overcome historical collecting practices where objects were removed from their social and cultural contexts. However, indigenous communities have not all experienced positive benefits of the new museology; as Wilson argues, "The cultural base of a museum is about power . . . it's the glorification of theft, because most of it is theft. They just collect and acquire. Acquire is just a flash word for pinching" (personal communication, 12 December 2013). Wilson however, recognises that museums are changing and providing new opportunities for indigenous peoples.

In New Zealand museums an indigenous museology is evident today which, as Geismar (2013, p. 130) describes, "prioritises the need to incorporate indigenous perspectives and recognizes indigenous priority in establishing representational conventions." Perspectives and representations such as these are embedded in practice at Te Papa through the corporate principle of Mana Taonga that defines Māori participation and involvement. This principle recognises the spiritual and cultural connections of taonga with their people through whakapapa (genealogy) (Schorch & Hakiwai, 2014, p. 15). Scholars Schorch and Hakiwai (2014) further argue that drawing on indigenous thought rather than only Western theory when employing a cross-cultural collaborative process contributes to "a more democratic form of knowledge production" in the museum (ibid., p. 13). Taking this experience of museum thought and practice from one familiar network (in New Zealand) and transposing it to another network, less familiar and located elsewhere (in England), through this project with Ngā Paerangi iwi provided an opportunity for critical reflection on cross-cultural collaboration as effected across geographic distance.

In November 2013, nine members of the iwi (introduced in Chapter 1) travelled the 19,000 km to the Pitt Rivers Museum in Oxford, England to meet their taonga and establish a relationship with museum staff on behalf of Ngā Paerangi (Figure 2.2). This was a momentous undertaking for all members of this group. Although some were seasoned travellers, age, health, distance and the emotional strain of such an undertaking affected them all. Some of the group, having never travelled outside of New Zealand, were especially overwhelmed by the distance.

Staff members at the Pitt Rivers Museum hosted the Ngā Paerangi group: Jeremy Coote, curator for Oceanic and African Collections and joint head of collections; Laura Peers, curator for Americas Collections; Chris Morton, curator for Photograph and Manuscript Collections; Madeleine Ding, Faye Belsey and Zena McGreevy, assistant curators; Heather Richardson, head of conservation; Kate Jackson, conservator. Zena McGreevy also had

Figure 2.2 Ngā Paerangi group with Jeremy Coote at Pitt Rivers Museum, 2013.
Photo by Michelle Horwood.

relatives among the Ngā Paerangi group. These staff have had considerable experience hosting individuals and groups from originating communities. The Ngā Paerangi visit, however, was the first research visit from a Māori tribal group from New Zealand for current museum staff.

Based upon prior experience with other indigenous groups and discussions with the author, Coote and Peers suggested an informal ('low key') welcome for the Ngā Paerangi group involving introductions to staff and museum procedures. This would be a balance between Ngā Paerangi expectations and museum practicalities. Peers also suggested using the model adopted for a previous visit by members of the Haida Nation in 2009, where "the more staff members you can involve and get to take a sort of professional and personal investment in the project the better" (personal communication, 12 November 2013). Providing opportunities for relationships to be established between individual staff and members of the Ngā Paerangi group was considered the most likely way for long-term outcomes to result. Coote also suggested that Ngā Paerangi enter the museum through a neutral space (Robinson Close side entrance of the museum building leading into a seminar room) rather than through the galleries, as he was concerned the group might feel confronted or overwhelmed by some of the displays (Peers & Coote, personal communication, 3 November 2013). Furthermore, Peers explicitly requested no filming of the welcome occasion as it would be "intrusive and make staff feel self-conscious" (personal communication, 14 November 2013).

The karanga (ceremonial call of welcome) from Ngā Paerangi kuia accompanied our approach to the museum entry where we were met by staff who escorted us to the side entrance and into the building. Once inside introductions were exchanged, followed by an object handling session. The welcome concluded with lunch in the Blackwood Room, a room set aside for the exclusive use of Ngā Paerangi during their visit.

Five days were spent with taonga from the Charles Smith collection. Research and storerooms were ritually cleared by karakia (prayer) and karanga on first entering them. Ngā Paerangi were respectful of handling procedures for object and human safety. Four or five staff accompanied Ngā Paerangi at all times when with taonga to ensure safety of objects and to provide assistance if needed, such as handling advice. A strategy was put in place following damage to one object to minimise the risk of any further damage occurring (Figure 2.3). A farewell ceremony concluded the visit with speeches, waiata and gift exchanges.

Preparation of objects for viewing was well planned and coordinated. Full access was given for all items requested. These were made available in small groups in the collection research room. Once examination was complete, the material was returned to a transit store and a new group of items brought out. Detailed information about each object was recorded; measurements were taken, materials identified, manufacturing processes described. The taonga were also photographed and additional information to that available on the museum's collection database noted. Most of the larger textile items were off-site, requiring a trip to this storage facility.

Meeting the tūpuna

As stated in the Protocol Agreement developed with the museum, "Ngā Paerangi see these taonga as an enduring living legacy between their tūpuna (ancestors) and current and future generations." On the first day, after a morning of greeting and conversation, Ngā Paerangi were therefore understandably anxious to see the taonga they had come so far to meet. Wīpaki Peeti led the way into the research room where the taonga had been placed, with his daughter Teresa Peeti behind him and the rest of the group following. He recited a karakia on approaching the room and entering it that lasted

Figure 2.3 Pitt Rivers Museum staff, from left Connor Tulloch and Jeremy Coote, with Haimona Rzoska and Tuata Angus observing Heather Richardson providing object handling advice, 2013.

Photo by Michelle Horwood.

several minutes. Katrina Hāwira followed this with a karanga. We were then able to enter the room. The group had requested that the taonga directly linked to the families of those present should be the first to be viewed. Therefore, Te Oti Takarangi's taiaha and tewhatewha (weapons/symbols of authority), hei (pendant), and tā moko (tattoo) taonga as well as the hamana (cartouche case), heru (comb) and hoeroa (symbol of authority/staff) were waiting in the room when we entered.

After thirty minutes of looking closely at taonga, Hera Pēina and Wīpaki Peeti moved to one corner to sit and talk. They were reminiscing about people and places. They remained seated for the rest of the session and all the group migrated regularly to sit with them and talk. They were like an anchor to return to when a break from direct engagement with the taonga was needed. Once the group had settled into examining, admiring and reflecting about taonga the anxiety of the previous few hours had lifted and everyone's emotions had calmed down. During the subsequent days the group became

Figure 2.4 Reti Wisneski, Katrina Hāwira and Wīpaki Peeti, with Kate Jackson, conservator, behind, Pitt Rivers Museum, 2013.

Photo by Michelle Horwood.

very relaxed with the museum staff and were happy to share information about taonga or traditional practices, such as eel fishing, with the staff and with each other.

As a result of this visit, Chris Morton had the photographs in the collection digitised and uploaded to the museum's database where they could be downloaded by family members.

Figure 2.5 Reti Wisneski and Katrina Hāwira, Pitt Rivers Museum, 2013.
Photo by Michelle Horwood.

Figure 2.6 Viewing kākahu cloaks, Pitt Rivers Museum, 2013.
Photo by Teresa Peeti.

Talking it over

> I think the perpetuity is embedded in the objects . . . that's where that rela-
> tionship is.
>
> Jeremy Coote[4]

During the Pitt Rivers Museum visit, time was set aside for the Ngā Paerangi group and museum staff, represented by Jeremy Coote and Heather Richardson, to meet to discuss ways in which the relationship between them could be developed and perpetuated. All present had an opportunity to make their opinions known and constructively contribute to the discussion. This centred on access to/restricting knowledge, opportunities for the future and defining a suitable timeframe for these, and collective responsibilities.

Within the museum, staff manaakitanga (hospitality, support) had ensured a positive and memorable experience for members of Ngā Paerangi. As a result it was suggested at this hui that a formal outcome might not be necessary because of the 'trust and aroha' (love) developed over the week at the museum. Coote agreed, stating that pieces of paper were acceptable, but it was people who made relationships, and these relationships were reinforced by being together (ibid.). However, in my experience working with communities, documents are useful in that they are more binding than verbal agreements, and they identify mutually agreed achievable outcomes and timeframes. Māori tribal groups are also familiar with working in this way through the Waitangi Tribunal processes, for example.

Coote also pointed out that the Protocol Agreement embodied his feelings about how the museum operated, especially the idea of reciprocity. However, they were still working through what would happen next, with regard to the future of their relationship. He thought a public outcome would be good, such as a journal article with Ngā Paerangi contributing. In response Takahia Tawaroa suggested the outcomes of the visit could be produced as *Taku Whare E* volume 4.[5] This is a clear articulation of parallel (or polar opposite) opinions about communication and benefits, where one outcome would be accessible to the academy while the other would be accessible to the tribal community. As Sully (2007, p. 31) states, regarding authority of the academy and the subservience of other world views, recipients of knowledge were Western scholars and audiences, rarely was knowledge produced for consumption by the subject. However, the suggestions did trigger discussion about possibilities for wider distribution of information about the collection through publication or web-based opportunities, including educational benefits for schools in New Zealand.

The most important outcome for Ngā Paerangi was the potential for the taonga to come to New Zealand, accompanied by museum staff to embed the embryonic relationships developed in Oxford. Coote agreed that a good first step for this to occur would be for staff to visit Kaiwhāiki. All considered a two- to three-year timeframe optimum.

The museum visit concluded with a gift exchange ceremony in the Blackwood Room with all the staff present who had helped to host the Ngā Paerangi group over the week. Speeches were made and koha (gifts) presented to the staff and volunteers who had provided manaakitanga, as well as to the museum. Pēina read and presented a letter from Kaiwhāiki Pā Trust on behalf of Ngā Paerangi, formally inviting staff of the museum to Kaiwhāiki. The aim of the invitation was to strengthen their relationship, provide staff with an insight into the community from where the taonga had originated, and to reciprocate the hospitality shown to the group in Oxford. The museum staff then replied and presented gifts in return. Final farewells were made and we all departed the museum.

Final observations

Museum staff facilitated full access to the Charles Smith collection during the 2013 visit. At this time, 122 items were viewed and documented. Ngā Paerangi engagement with their material heritage was observed and recorded. Interviews with five museum staff were completed by the author, and there was an open discussion between staff and Ngā Paerangi members about the experiences during the visit, and opportunities for continuing the relationship into the future.

During the course of the week at Oxford, individual members of Ngā Paerangi had responded to being with the taonga in different ways. The museum visit was initially an overwhelming experience combining sadness with awe and excitement. This progressed over the course of the week to enthusiastic engagement, reflection and discussion. Connections between the taonga and people in the past and today were central to all conversations, while opportunities arose to embed individual taonga within personal/ family narratives. Individuals used personal experience with and knowledge of materials, tools and activities to contextualise taonga they encountered within tribal practices; for example hīnaki (eel trap) and fishing, poi (percussion instrument) and kapa haka. There were also many opportunities to reflect on the Whanganui River, its centrality to tribal life, the resources the river provides, and how this was manifest in many items in the collection. There was consensus from the Ngā Paerangi group that all had gone well with the visit.

In their own words: interviews with iwi members and museum staff

In the previous chapter, archival research provided the context for a contemporary exploration of the meaning of items within an historical collection to a community and a museum. This was achieved through qualitative interviews with key informants from Ngā Paerangi iwi and members of the Pitt Rivers Museum staff, hui/focus groups and participant observation. A number of findings arose from the analysis of this data.

A key responsibility for museums in the twenty-first century is to provide access to the collections and associated information in their care. Coote concurred when he stated,

> the first responsibility of the museum is to look after what it's got, the second is to know what it's got, and the third is to know what it knows about what it's got, and the fourth is to make that information available to everybody.
>
> (Coote, personal communication, 15 November 2013)

Until the advent of online databases (2006 for the Pitt Rivers Museum) the 'everybody' referred to here was restricted to those who could physically visit the institution or who received a response from museum staff following enquiries about the museum's holdings. Museums at home or abroad, however, have generally remained inaccessible to Māori, with the exception of whānau (family) or hapū (sub-tribal) groups who have established individual relationships with institutions (and more usually individual staff members within institutions), based upon specific taonga. Te Whānau-a-Ruataupare's involvement with the Ruatepupuke whare whakairo (carved meeting house) at the Field Museum in Chicago illustrates this (Hakiwai, 1995).

A further finding relates to the survival of tangible and intangible cultural heritage. For Ngā Paerangi people, there was no expectation that significant taonga would have left the area and now exist in an overseas museum. The reasons for this are two-fold. Firstly, although the Whanganui Regional Museum has an important taonga collection of more than 4,500 items, and a significant proportion of these are from the Whanganui region, very few (four) are attributed to Ngā Paerangi (Horwood & Wilson, 2008). This suggests Ngā Paerangi people did not consider a museum a suitable repository for taonga and therefore did not lend or donate items to the local museum. Secondly, there is a general understanding that taonga from Ngā Paerangi were lost through warfare, fire and so forth or did not survive the passing of their owner; taonga were buried with their owner or placed in the river following their death, a practice that has continued to the present day. Consequently, Ngā Paerangi informants were delighted to know the Charles Smith collection was extant, a number expressing similar sentiments to Simon who commented, "the fact that they've been found to be existing is the surprise" (personal communication, 20 March 2013).

Rzoska explained one reason for the removal of taonga from the community, reflecting on past generations' predictions for the future in response to challenges and demands of a rapidly changing society.

> I think our old people actually thought . . . that the next generation wouldn't be able to handle those things. That's why a lot of those things were taken away and buried . . . if they need to come back they will be found.
>
> (personal communication, 20 March 2013)

Ponga concurred when she said, "you've got the taonga that were given back to the river. And I would like to think that those taonga were given back to keep us safe" (personal communication, 18 August 2013). She expanded on this idea, stating, that there was,

> this definite shift to leave the old with the old and to progress with the new . . . With their understanding that that was that time, that was that world, now we've got to look to the future . . . and we look at all those kōrero about our children being the taonga for the future. No whakairo, no carvings for the walls, because our children would represent the future and those stories [told in the carvings] would be maintained within the people. Unfortunately . . . a lot of those accounts were lost with those people and not necessarily passed down. And this is us today trying to struggle to get those taonga back, to reclaim historical events through research, through all of the types of things we are doing today.

Here Ponga is referring to the desire by her grandparents' and great grandparents' generations to focus upon the future and not the ways of the past, by removing the tangible evidence of past practices and histories. This resonates with Sissons' (2014) comprehensive account of the rapid conversion to Christianity of Polynesian societies during the nineteenth century. He suggests the evidence for the deliberate rejection of the traditional religious basis, which he terms the 'Polynesian Iconoclasm,' was the abandonment of old structures and the erection of new ones.

Indeed, the impact of colonisation had far-reaching social consequences throughout New Zealand: in the nineteenth century, these included changes in population health, literacy, intermarriage and economy as well as the effect on cultural values with the introduction of Christianity, emerging Māori nationalism, and altered tribal alliances as a result of access to new technology and European allies. In Whanganui Te Korenga (Kerehoma) Tūwhāwhākia of Kaiwhāiki recalled the terrifying effect of an epidemic called rewharewha arriving in Whanganui in the early nineteenth century where people died not singly, but in tens and twenties and thirties.[6] Depopulation as a result of epidemics such as this, as well as the contribution of warfare during the nineteenth century, and the progressive alienation of land, were exacerbated by assimilationist policies of the twentieth century resulting in cultural erosion where "much of incalculable value was lost" (Waitangi Tribunal, 2011, p. 14). Many of these factors have contributed to loss of knowledge for Ngā Paerangi with one consequence being the lack of survival of information within the tribe today about individual items in the Charles Smith collection, or the people associated with them.

Ponga's statement contrasts with Pitt Rivers Museum staff perspectives where their skills are used to decipher the collecting history of the items in their care. Central to Coote's view is that he sees it as his responsibility to

> unpick and unpack the past of objects in the collection . . . [then] by putting the collections out there, by publishing them, by exhibiting them, by putting them on the internet, etcetera, etcetera, it becomes possible for them to be properly connected to the past.
>
> (Coote, personal communication, 15 November 2013).

This is certainly sound professional practice for those responsible for cultural history collections. It has become more common practice, however, particularly for those museums that live alongside originating communities, to engage with these communities to contextualise this material from the outset. A further research finding therefore relates to prioritising relationships over research, and cultural knowledge as well as collecting histories. The following example illustrates some of the potential benefits of working with originating communities.

During a research seminar in Visual, Material and Museum Anthropology at Oxford, Coote presented students with a Māori tatā (canoe bailer) from the Forster Collection directing discussion to its function and origins. The session concluded with a video of Māori artist George Nuku together with Coote discussing the same object in which Nuku used a performative approach to enhance Coote's (and the viewers') understanding of the value of this taonga to him, as a member of the community from which it originated. While Coote's analysis focussed upon the physicality of the object, with attention first being drawn to a mend in the scoop, as well as his ability to unpack historical literary narratives, Nuku, conversely, paid no attention to any written history or use-wear but rather expounded on the meaning to him of the symbolic referencing in the object's shape and carved detail. He did not need to know that it was a part of the material collected during the second voyage of Captain Cook to New Zealand. Rather he described its potent imagery and tapu (sacred) nature and interpreted the object based upon symbols and values from his experience of the world; he is Māori, a carver and an artist. His mind took him elsewhere when he looked at the object; he put it in context – on a waka tauā (war canoe) – which opened up a whole range of meanings associated with war and waka and why it was so heavily decorated. He discussed the trinity of tangata (people), whare (house), waka (canoe) which is embodied in the tatā as they are similarly in a waka and stated that "[t]hey don't symbolise those things, they *are* those things." He was determined to communicate meaning: the symbolism of the fertility implied by the handle/male/procreation and the scoop/female/vessel. He related how such tatā are all named and passed on, so are therefore as potent as the waka they accompany. It was clear that for Nuku, space and time collapsed when he encountered taonga, as they link back to ancestors, as experienced and described by Tapsell (2006, 2011).

Nuku's encounter with the tatā was a valuable opportunity for this group of anthropology students to gain a glimpse into a Māori world view. It also told far more than Coote will ever be able to through his archival research, and certainly highlights the value of a cross-disciplinary and cross-cultural analysis of ethnographic items, as argued by Schorch and Hakiwai (2014), which could go some way to countering Ngā Paerangi's loss of intimate knowledge of their taonga. As Sully (2007, p. 28) points out, Western knowledge systems privilege European perspectives and displace alternative world views and "[e]mbedded within this is the credibility given to the historical and ethnographic records of European scholars over indigenous oral histories that marginalise knowledge systems of non-Europeans." Coote did not consider the video recording of this dialogue with Nuku as potentially a valuable addition to the Pitt Rivers Museum website, to expand the information currently available online from Coote's historical and museum history research. Therefore, access to this type of information experienced and recorded by the museum is very limited. He was uncomfortable with this dialogue as it was not a pre-scripted, pre-planned recording and he was concerned about the suitability of some of the commentary or lack of it. He described his responsibility and research focus with the collection as having,

primarily been on their identification and their history . . . leaving questions of meaning and significance and symbolism to the specialists, and in the specialists the knowledge holders in the communities from which the objects come. And I'm quite happy and content at doing that. I don't feel that I'm not doing part of my job by not knowing and not putting into the public domain all the cultural knowledge relevant to all 300,000 objects in the collection.

(Coote, personal communication, 15 November 2013)

World views

Insight into how the different world views of participants contributed to the evolving meshwork of relationships and actions affecting the taonga in the Charles Smith collection, was possible from research findings, and clarified the divergent positions of Ngā Paerangi and Pitt Rivers Museum staff on the importance of indigenous museum collections. From an indigenous perspective K. Clarke, for example, refers to human remains as, "it might be one hundred years dead but it's still like a grandmother yesterday, it's still that grieving process that we would go through" (personal communication, 26 July 2013). Conversely, Coote placed value on current action, "the past is really interesting, intrinsically interesting, but it doesn't have value, because it's gone. The value is the future" (personal communication, 15 November 2013). He did, however, see similarity in his use of ethnographic collections with Māori

> ideas about the animacy of objects and the increasing mana of objects as they pass from one owner to another . . . [as this] fits with my museological approach which is tracing the history of objects and what's been done with them. So that I find that my work . . . actually fits reasonably well with at least parts of the Māori idea about objects.
>
> (ibid.)

He also articulated his view of the museum's role in extending the lives of the objects when he said,

> there's sometimes the perception that . . . the object dies when it goes to a museum and nothing happens and they're forgotten about . . . But . . . objects are continually being looked at again and again; being brought out for researchers, or prepared for display . . . it's what makes the collections alive.
>
> (ibid.)

Coote did acknowledge that a major influence on anthropological thought and literature related to meanings of the gift and Māori ideas about the life force of objects and associated concepts through the work of Marcel Mauss (1954), and, as a result, this had influenced his approach to working with indigenous material heritage. Consequently, he believes that there is continuity in the life of an object; its story does not stop at the moment it is removed from an indigenous framework, and a new one start when it enters a Western collecting paradigm. "It's actually the same story; the way Māori look at that and the way I look at that are not necessarily incongruent" (ibid.).

While animacy of the object is one entity revealed through this analysis, another is cultural knowledge, access to it, and how its deployment contributes to an understanding of the distribution of power across this heritage network. Ngā Paerangi informants, for example, provided a number of reasons for withholding cultural knowledge. Rzoska considered it dependent "on what the person wants that knowledge for. I've no problems about giving out to anybody, but if I think they're really not there for the right reason I wouldn't bother" (personal communication, 20 March 2013). Simon agreed, "It's not just given; . . . you shoulder tap certain ones to take the knowledge on" (personal communication, 20 March 2013). He continued, using the examples of music composition and performance, speech making and genealogy, "I was told by my uncle, that you stay with the music, you stay with the kōrero . . . whakapapa, you leave that to someone else. Well it took another generation, down to Haimona, but he's picked it up very well." Here Simon is emphasising that individuals are recognised and encouraged when they show a particular predisposition or talent for a specific activity. Wilson also emphasised that there is no set rule as to what knowledge is restricted as it depends on the situation.

> it's important to never be taught rules . . . You have to be taught values and principles. So you can then make a sound decision based upon the circumstances before you. The olds were quite clear when they were teaching me. "No good giving you a rule book boy!" Because every tangi [funeral] is different, every hui is different.
> (personal communication, 12 December 2013)

Museum staff expanded upon changing museum practices that take into account sensitivities regarding cultural knowledge transfer. Uden, for example, commented,

> some cultural knowledge isn't ours to have . . . I think in the last few years we understand that sometimes that cultural knowledge is only

given to certain people and people don't have the authority to share it with us and even if they did they might not want to.

(personal communication, 6 November 2013)

Peers endorsed this stating,

We don't have the right to capture all information about objects. We don't have the right to dictate what kinds of projects necessarily occur with our collections that we care for. Other people may have those rights, right now, and you just have to recognise that.

(personal communication, 12 November 2013)

Although conflicted in this area, Coote believed he had worked through a tenable solution.

I find being at a university institution in which pursuit and sharing knowledge are the prime values, one has to find ways of dealing with those issues, that are respectful to people who have different views, but also respect the traditions of a free and open society . . . we would not refuse permission, we would explain to anybody asking for access to Tasmanian material in the collection [for example] what the view of the Tasmanian Aboriginal Council was, and that seemed to me to be the only reasonable solution to that situation.

(Coote, personal communication, 15 November 2013)

In a similar vein several museum informants unsurprisingly felt no particular obligation to initiate contact with originating communities owing to the nature and scale of the museum's collections. As Richardson stated, "I don't think we have the capacity to go out and find all those communities" (personal communication, 6 November 2013). Rather, they try to make items accessible through online resources and other media and are happy to work with these communities if approached by them. Coote added, "ideally if there were no limits to the museum's resources then we would be delighted to be proactive about developing relationships that we are always happy to be reactive to" (personal communication, 15 November 2013). Peers, however, suggested a more proactive approach is important. With regard to museum obligations to originating communities she commented,

You have to tell the people you've got the stuff. [Laughs.] And not just by putting it up on the web and saying that, that is access. You have to figure out which communities you need to go to. You have to be proactive about alerting those communities to the presence of those collections in the museum. And you have to be open to working with communities in whatever ways they choose or not . . . So you've got to be willing to work outside your comfort zone as a curator. You don't get to hide in your office . . . You've actually got to go to your community.

(personal communication, 12 November 2013)

Once connection has been achieved, she further noted, every effort is made to accommodate "individuals with particular genealogical connections to objects." With regard to the Charles Smith collection, Coote and Peers both emphasised its specialness due to its associated provenance data, Peers adding, "in some ways we value the documentation associated as much as we value the objects themselves."

Ngā Paerangi valued reengaging with their taonga through the actions of their ancestors, Charles Smith and his descendants, as Ngā Paerangi would not have had any of the taonga or knowledge of their existence if they had not been given to Smith and eventually reached the Pitt Rivers Museum collection. Also that the museum staff were exemplary in their care of the taonga. While the importance of the retention of the knowledge about the gifting relationships central to these transactions cannot be understated, there were few suggestions as to why these taonga would have been gifted or sold to Smith. Simon suggested that, "oftentimes they did things that were a reciprocation of something else" (personal communication, 20 March 2013). Rzoska also thought that, "they must've had some sort of connection with him that actually made them feel that they were able to give him things or sell him things" (personal communication, 5 December 2013).

Identification of indigenous agency in the assembling of collections such as this has potential for providing insight into these historical relationships of collectors, museums and communities and it was possible to identify a number of the strategies Ngā Paerangi members employed to facilitate the gift exchanges and trade opportunities from which Smith's collection developed. These included strengthening relationships, removing dangerous goods from the community, obtaining social status and profit, producing replicas and inventing new items. Assigning primacy to the processes of collection formation rather than to the collection as it exists has been beneficial in drawing attention to the ways in which the historical network constituents interacted. It illustrated social and political activity contributing to understanding intertribal relationships during the mid-nineteenth century in the central North Island of New Zealand, and framed contemporary relationships development during recent fieldwork. It was also possible to document the objectification of relationships between network constituents as well as the transformation of the object from a passive thing to an active actor-entity.

Figure 2.7 'Coming to sell curios' Ngā Paerangi elders and Tāmati Takarangi (wearing korowai) at Charles Smith's house, Te Korito, Whanganui River, around 1885 to 1890.

Copyright Pitt Rivers Museum, University of Oxford; 1998.243.4.8.

The final entity that emerged from the analysis of this network relates to authority over decision-making. Pitt Rivers Museum staff were unified in their willingness to privilege originating communities' authority over decision-making regarding their cultural heritage. Peers describes one example, "we have taken things off display because people from the communities felt it wasn't appropriate to display them" (personal communication, 12 November 2013). Efforts are also made to enable access to originating community perspectives about the collection, as she continues, "what we are really trying to record on the database is indigenous community perspectives and understandings. We always say to people 'What do you want us to know to put on the database?'" However, they have 'chosen to maintain' (ibid.) the historical display approach now considered to be "different approaches to how things are made" rather than "the evolution of form from the primitive to the more civilised" (Belsey, personal communication, 12 November 2013). Coote further articulated this when he described his perception of visitors' responses to the museum,

after people have visited the museum they can often have quite a different feeling about it, because of its universality and its lack of cultural apartheid. And if people get what the museum is about, which isn't a colonial racist view of the world but is about celebrating human creativity and ingenuity and putting all cultures on the same level of creativity and ingenuity and historicity then they're not as worried as they were before they came.

(personal communication, 15 November 2013)

This certainly was true for the Ngā Paerangi group, although it may also have been a case of being overwhelmed by the displays – the diversity and volume of material on display.

I would suggest, however, that what Peers and Coote described (the museum staff's willingness to privilege the authority of cultural groups and concepts implicit in the philosophy of the museum), is not explicit in the approach to the display of items to the general public who visit the museum. There are exceptions, such as those visitors experiencing specific museum events. The method of display has meant, as Coote considers, "That we're sort of let off the hook!" from "pursuing the cultural significance and cultural meaning" in the public interpretation of the collections (personal communication, 15 November 2013). As his colleagues have stated, public and non-public faces of the museum expose different professional sensibilities (Harris & O'Hanlon, 2013, p. 10). Furthermore, the temporary character of a museum public programmes, and their affective nature, are not often visible via an institution's website or publications.

Worlds apart

While world views can account for differing priorities for and engagements with indigenous heritage items, understanding that distance between the human actors in this heritage network is more than a physical phenomenon, is contributed to by their divergent positions on a number of emerging issues. Museum staff recognised a number of outcomes for the museum including the value of new skills they might acquire for care of taonga. Also,

to help future researchers, to know more about the objects . . . one useful outcome would be for us to enhance the database records for those objects . . . Another would be to establish longer term contacts for community group members so that if we have insufficient information we have somebody to turn to . . . And having a sense that we're no longer strangers to the community that we do have a relationship with them is also an important outcome for us . . . We have research requests from all over the world . . . We need help responding to those, we recognise that we are not the ultimate authority on that anymore.

(Peers, personal communication, 12 November 2013)

On the other hand, Peers did indicate that she privileged knowledge that could come into the museum and enhance the collection when she stated that,

> there needs to be a lot more genealogy done. I think the community needs to be involved in that . . . we need to understand much more about [Charles Smith] and his relationships with Māori people. And about why Māori people would have transferred the material to him.
>
> (ibid.)

There was consensus among Ngā Paerangi informants on the range of outcomes possible from reconnecting with these taonga and establishing a relationship with the museum. The welfare of the taonga was, however, at the centre of their concerns, articulated in terms of enhancing cultural safety for the taonga and those who encountered them by sharing cultural knowledge with staff. Importantly, this would be a two-way relationship of mutual benefit. Developing this relationship as well as (tribal and institutional) commitment to this relationship in the long-term was a primary objective of this visit to Oxford for Ngā Paerangi and this was explicitly stated in the Protocol Agreement forwarded to the museum prior to the visit. Coote however felt that,

> committing the community as it continues to exist through time, and the museum as it exists is all well and good, but it's only a piece of paper. What's really going to matter is what people do, and what they do is going to really be based on their relationships.
>
> (personal communication, 15 November 2013)

And Peers clearly articulated the museum's position,

> We don't generally do those kinds of documents . . . And that's useful in many ways, in that it allows a greater latitude of relationships and conversations . . . It's actually more flexible and stronger if you have a whole variety of people in the community that the museum can contact, and a whole variety of people the community can contact here . . . we can agree that we recognise the community's involvement in a collection without putting that on a piece of paper . . . We recognise the broad relationship between the collection, the museum and the community. That may be as far as we go.
>
> (personal communication, 12 November 2013)

Coote also observed, "We have a relationship; it's implicit in the objects . . . If it's going to develop that depends upon projects" (personal communication, 15 November 2013). To maintain this embryonic relationship, for the museum to pay attention to Ngā Paerangi's wish to engage with their taonga and the museum, active and ongoing conversations are therefore required to initiate a project. Bearing in mind that, as Coote states, "the visit and the Protocol Agreement helps to put the collection at the forefront of people's minds at the museum, but there's lots of other things continually beating at the museum's door" (ibid.). Similarly, for Ngā Paerangi at this time, with the Waitangi Tribunal Whanganui River Settlement process at a crucial stage, a leadership change with the death of Morvin Simon, and major capital developments in progress at Kaiwhāiki marae, their resources are also spread in many directions.

At the same time Ponga clearly articulated Ngā Paerangi people's desire to be introspective first and think solely of their needs in relation to the taonga that they were re-encountering, rather than consider the formalities of the human relationships, and from this everything else would smoothly result. It was imperative, however, for staff to provide this opportunity in the first instance. As she concluded,

> if they can see that connection from us as a people, not just to the tangible taonga itself, but it's the spiritual, it's the wairua connection to those people who used them . . . then hopefully they will get a bigger understanding of what those taonga mean to us.
>
> (personal communication, 18 August 2013)

Museum staff, to the best of their abilities, respectfully endeavoured to accommodate this request.

While repatriation discussions would not be a part of this visit to Oxford, it was still difficult for Ngā Paerangi members to think beyond this urgent need to have these taonga back 'home' where they could be appropriately cared for and reinserted into tribal narratives through direct encounter. As Simon stated, when identifying the best outcome for the taonga, it "would have to be . . . at home, it would not be as appropriate as being appropriately looked after at a museum close to home . . . and . . . a Paerangi to be looking after it" (personal communication, 20 March 2013). Furthermore, Rzoska could not reconcile their lack of taonga in Kaiwhāiki with what seemed a surplus in Oxford, more than could be displayed.

> What's the use of them being put away for no one to see? I know I'd rather see them being given back to the families that they might've belonged to before to use them, than to be sitting in the dungeon doing nothing . . . ideally for me I would love to see all those things, no matter what condition they're in, being displayed.
>
> (Rzoska, personal communication, 20 March 2013)

This ideal, however, conflicts with museum best practice where the use made of an item cannot compromise its physical safety. The display method at the Pitt Rivers Museum – a comparative technology approach rather than a geographic or cultural arrangement – also took the Ngā Paerangi group by surprise who would have liked, as T Peeti noted, "to see all the Māori objects all together" (personal communication, 21 January 2014). Whereas, by maintaining the present public interface, Coote suggested,

> we do not perhaps pursue the cultural significance and cultural mean-
> ing, and the symbolism, etcetera that one would expect to find in other
> museums because most of the objects are displayed by their function
> rather than in a cultural display.
>
> (personal communication, 15 November 2013)

In recent years, however, museum staff have used short-term exhibitions and related events to contextualise particular items and collections.

Conclusion

In this chapter I presented the results of face-to-face encounters of all assemblage components at the centre of this study, the Charles Smith collection, the Ngā Paerangi community and the Pitt Rivers Museum, supplemented by interviews with museum staff and community members, and participant observation. I also posed a number of questions against the research findings based around themes of distance, ownership, access and engagement.

The effects of these encounters, which involved object handling sessions and hui, suggest benefits that might arise when a museum and an originating community invest in building a relationship between them. The disassembling and analysis of the separate components through a range of methods in this and the preceding chapter has provided an opportunity to consider the impact of other assemblages that surround and interact with those at the centre of this investigation. Furthermore, a number of entities emerged from the analysis of this assemblage, including ideas of object and indigenous agency, access to cultural knowledge, and authority over decision-making. These results also revealed the disparate cultural perspectives of the two groups and how awareness of these differences can enhance our understanding of the past and present life of the objects for the community and museum. In the next chapter these findings are discussed by way of a number of emergent themes centred on time and place, power and values.

Notes

1 Personal communication, 20 March 2013.
2 Ngā Paerangi iwi and museum staff generously accommodated a timeframe constrained by a three-year doctoral research programme.
3 A reference to humility (Brougham, Reed, & Kāretu, 2012, p. 93).
4 Personal communication, 15 November 2013.
5 *Taku Whare E* volumes 1–3 by Morvin Simon are an anthology of marae past and present throughout the Whanganui and Rangitīkei regions.
6 National Library of New Zealand; MS-Papers-1187–190. This epidemic is likely to have been influenza for which Māori populations had no natural defences.

References

Allen, L., & Hamby, L. (2011). Pathways to knowledge: Research, agency and power relations in the context of collaborations between museums and source communities. In S. Byrne, A. Clarke, R. Harrison, & R. Torrence (Eds.), *Unpacking the collection: Museums, identity and agency* (pp. 209–229). New York: Springer.

Atkinson, J. K. (2014). *Education, values and ethics in international heritage: Learning to respect.* Farnham: Ashgate Publishing Ltd.

Bolton, L., Thomas, N., Bonshek, E., Adams, J., & Burt, B. (2013). *Melanesia: Art and encounter.* London: The British Museum Press.

Brougham, A. E., Reed, A. W., & Kāretu, T. S. (2012). *The Raupō book of Māori proverbs* (5th ed.). Auckland: Raupo.

de Stecher, A., & Loyer, S. (2009). Practising collaborative research: The Great Lakes Research Alliance visits to the Pitt Rivers Museum and British Museum. *Journal of Museum Ethnography, 22,* 145–154.

Geismar, H. (2013). *Treasured possessions: Indigenous interventions into cultural and intellectual property.* Durham: Duke University Press.

Hakiwai, A. (1995). Ruatepupuke: Working together, understanding one another. *New Zealand Museums Journal, 25*(1), 42–44.

Harris, C., & O'Hanlon, M. (2013). The future of the enthnographic museum. *Anthropology Today, 29*(1), 8–12.

Horwood, M. (2017). Going digital in the GLAM sector: ICT innovations & collaborations for taonga Māori. In H. Whaanga, M. Apperley, & T. T. Keegan (Eds.), *Te whare hangarau Māori: Language, culture and technology* (pp. 149–164). Hamilton: University of Waikato.

Horwood, M., & Wilson, C. (2008). *Te ara tapu, sacred journeys: Whanganui Regional Museum taonga Māori collection.* Auckland: Random House.

Kreps, C. F. (2003). Curatorship as social practice. *Curator: The Museum Journal, 46*(3), 311–323.

Krmpotich, C., Peers, L. L., Haida Repatriation Committee, & staff of the Pitt Rivers Museum and British Museum. (2013). *This is our life: Haida material heritage and changing museum practice.* Vancouver: University of British Columbia Press.

Lyons, N., Hennessy, K., Arnold, C., & Joe, M. (2011). *The Inuvialuit Smithsonian Project: Winter 2009-Spring 2011*. Retrieved from www.irc.inuvialuit.com/publications/pdf/Inuvialuit%20Smithsonian%20Report.pdf.

Mauss, M. (1954). *The gift*. London: Cohen and West.

Onciul, B. (2013). Community engagement, curatorial practice, and museum ethos in Alberta, Canada. In V. Golding & W. Modest (Eds.), *Museums and communities: Curators, collections and collaboration* (pp. 79–97). London: Bloomsbury.

Patterson, J. (1992). *Exploring Maori values*. Palmerston North: Dunmore Press.

Schorch, P., & Hakiwai, A. (2014). Mana taonga and the public sphere: A dialogue between indigenous practice and western theory. *International Journal of Cultural Studies, 17*(2), 191–205.

Sissons, J. (2014). *The Polynesian iconoclasm: Religious revolution and the seasonality of power*. New York: Berghahn Books.

Sully, D. (2007). *Decolonising conservation: Caring for Maori meeting houses outside New Zealand*. Walnut Creek, CA: Left Coast Press.

Tapsell, P. (2006). *Ko tawa: Maori treasures of New Zealand*. Auckland: David Bateman.

Tapsell, P. (2011). "Aroha mai: Whose museum?" The rise of indigenous ethics within museum contexts: A Maori-tribal perspective. In J. Marstine (Ed.), *Routledge companion to museum ethics: Redefining ethics for the twenty-first century museum* (pp. 85–111). London: Routledge.

Waitangi Tribunal. (2011). *Ko Aotearoa tēnei: A report into claims concerning New Zealand law and policy affecting Māori culture and identity, te taumata tuatahi, WAI262 Waitangi Tribunal Report*. Wellington: Legislation Direct.

3   Emergent themes from the disassembly-reassembly of a heritage network

Under-representation of an indigenous voice "in both scholarly and public discourse on museums and in the professional museum and anthropological community" (Kreps, 2011, p. 81) is one factor that can limit indigenous opportunities to engage with the museum-based custodians of their heritage and to establish ongoing relationships with them. Lack of affiliation with an academic or other cultural institution that can facilitate contact and communication, and disadvantages in terms of human, fiscal, technological and educational resources are also influential factors. Moreover, changes in museum practice are most advanced in countries where indigenous communities "live among settler-founded, modern nation-states" (Peers & Brown, 2003, p. 14) in relation to indigenous collections and authority over them. In this chapter I argue that these changes potentially provide models for adaptation elsewhere.

Through a case study grounded in a specific context, this investigation set out to explore the ways in which a Māori community in New Zealand could build a relationship with a university museum in England when they are separated by distance and, using an assemblage approach, identify ways to reconnect the community with items of their ancestral heritage that they had been separated from for more than a century. Examining the different cultural perspectives of the museum and the community over time furthers our understanding of the meaning of the heritage items to both groups today and how this might enable change in the relationships between them.

Three broad themes emerged from the analyses of assemblage components in the previous chapters that contribute to understanding how this might be possible. These emergent themes or entities include specific temporalities and places, manifestations of power (reflecting both priorities and resources), and differences in value systems which, together with a rethinking of historical collections and their development, enable their reassembly into new networks centred on enhanced relationships encompassing knowledge, respect and opportunities.

Times and places

While components of this study may be literally a world apart, a detailed examination reveals a network of events and effects that spans time and space, and draws the components together by effectively developing relationships between them. Of particular interest are the events that occurred during the period Charles Smith was acquiring items of material heritage from Ngā Paerangi, those events resulting from the recent rediscovery of the collection, and the effects on human and non-human agents of these events in the past, present and potentially in the future. Furthermore, as Hodder (2003, p. 165) discusses, new or contested meanings become apparent once a study such as this embraces temporal and spatial factors. The hoeroa, Ngā Karu o Niu Tīreni in the Charles Smith collection, for example, moved from being a statement of authority and power, to a means of reparation, to a symbol of alliance and emblem of political resistance, to a sign of colonial domination, then a representation of the 'Other,' and now an instantiation of an ancestor. As Tapsell (2006, p. 17) states, "taonga are time travellers that bridge the generations, enabling descendants to ritually meet their ancestors face to face." Tapsell (2006, 2011) also describes the meaning of taonga to whānau, hapū and iwi in relation to the maintenance of historical narratives; this is pertinent to the contextualisation of taonga over time. Here I discuss how analysis of the historical components of this relational network enable a collapsing of distance in space-time to provide insights into changing cultural perspectives between Māori tribal communities in New Zealand and museum staff in England over time, and in turn how this can influence the nature of the relationship between them.

Moreover, in considering changes in museum anthropology over the past three decades, in response to the assertion of rights to heritage management by indigenous groups and the unevenness in time and place of the decolonising process (Kreps, 2011, p. 80), I will compare current practices in museums in New Zealand and England with specific reference to the Pitt Rivers Museum and the author's experience at the Whanganui Regional Museum.

A final point from Tapsell (1997, p. 345) relates to reasons for the abandonment of taonga in the mid- to late-nineteenth century, in particular land alienation and kin-group identity loss. This resulted in taonga becoming "redundant, and many were eagerly acquired by waiting curio-hunters, collectors and museums."

There and then . . .

Although events before the arrival of Charles Smith in New Zealand in 1859 have resulted in effects that have impacted on assemblage components, the periods from the mid- to late-nineteenth century, when Smith acquired items, and when the collection received attention more recently from 2006 until today, delineate the temporal parameters of this study. Similarly, locations beyond Whanganui, New Zealand and Oxford, England will receive minimal attention. The challenges and opportunities faced by Smith and his Ngā Paerangi contacts are considered. As well the societal influences that prepared Smith for life in a settler colony, together with his Whanganui relationships, that contributed to the development of his collection. The effect of events that emerged in the early twenty-first century as a consequence of developments in online access to museum collections has been to inspire new events. In this case resulting in the contraction of the 19,000 kilometres of space separating the collection, its originating communities in New Zealand today, and the collection's current custodians in England. The importance of historical museum collections to indigenous peoples today is recognised, and it is acknowledged that they have an immensely important role as resources for the future.

A number of authors have elaborated on the universal concept of the past informing the future with especial reference to indigenous communities (for example, Clifford, 2004). "Kia whakatōmuri te haere whakamua" (I walk backwards into the future with my eyes fixed on my past) is a Māori proverb widely used in New Zealand to express the Māori concept of time. The following expands on this concept, providing insight into the complexities of the different epistemologies pertinent to this study.

> [Unlike] in English [where] the past is *behind* us, and the future is *ahead* of us . . . in Māori the past is **ngā rā o mua** (the days *ahead*) and the future is **ngā rā o muri** (the days *behind*) . . . From a Māori perspective time is not a path to be walked . . . it's a force like wind or water; you stay still, time moves . . . Your past has been seen therefore the past must be *in front of you* . . . But the future just sneaks up unknown and unseen, so the future is coming *from behind you*.
>
> (Anonymous, 2013)

This was the framework developed for the exhibition of nineteenth-century photographs of Whanganui Māori, *Te Pihi Mata – The Sacred Eye*, by Che Wilson, co-curator, where the photographs were seen as ". . . windows to the past connecting to tomorrow." He explains further,

> To Māori, images of their tūpuna are sacred treasures and a way of communicating with the past . . . They are alive, they are watching, they are listening. These people still reach out to us from a past that we may never physically know but which we can all spiritually feel.
>
> (Sharpe & Wilson, 2007)

Acknowledging validity of concepts such as this is central to decolonised museum practice and without which exhibitions such as *Te Pihi Mata* would not be possible. For this exhibition at Whanganui Regional Museum, employment of a Māori curator with authority to negotiate with and speak on behalf of Whanganui iwi, firmly embedded socially inclusive museum practice into an institution that had spearheaded governance reform in New Zealand within the principles of partnership and two cultures development arising from the Treaty of Waitangi (Butts, Dell, & Wills, 2002).

The taonga in the Charles Smith collection therefore provided the Ngā Paerangi community with a very special opportunity to be reunited with their ancestors in a way that had rarely been possible for them before. This was especially apparent at Oxford when the group first entered the space where the taonga were held. Although excited to have reached this long-anticipated moment of reconnection, they expressed a range of emotions from extreme anxiety to anger to amazement when first encountering the ihi (presence), wehi (awe) and wana (authority) of their ancestors. This was a new experience for most of the group, and the unfamiliar location (within an anthropology museum in a foreign country) required reliance on each other and learned tikanga to carry them through. I acknowledge that the museum had strategies in place for planned research visits by indigenous groups, as described in Chapter 2, providing the time and space for these encounters to take place.

Hera Pēina's request for photographs to be taken of her holding the taiaha Te Maungārongo which linked to her grandfather Īhaka Bailey and her Takarangi ancestors (Figure 3.1), further illustrates this. At the subsequent hui ā-iwi at Kaiwhāiki where the visit was reported back to the community, Pēina took the opportunity to talk to her relations about the significance of this moment for her. The genealogy of this taiaha, described in Chapter 1, identifies familial connections for Pēina's family which are reflected in names that have been passed to her family today. She reported that she had been overwhelmed by this opportunity to have her photograph taken holding this taonga and thus connecting directly with her ancestors. The taonga was not only a physical manifestation of these relationships but for Pēina validated her personal involvement in this project.

Another important finding that has emerged from the results relates to a conviction developed by Māori people during the second half of the nineteenth century and first half of the twentieth century, that to give up traditional practices and adopt European ones ('learning the Pākehā way') would be beneficial for advancement both for oneself and for one's children. To "progress their children to the future . . . there was definitely this shift to leave the old with the old and to progress with the new" (Ponga, personal communication, 18 August 2013). Tribal Māori did not anticipate

Figure 3.1 Hera Pēina holding Te Oti Takarangi's taiaha Te Maungārongo (Peace-maker), Pitt Rivers Museum, 2013.

Photo by Michelle Horwood.

Pākehā practices would become enforced through factors including assimi-lationist policies, urban migration and the consequences of land alienation. Of especial relevance to Ngā Paerangi, one impact of these changes was manifest in the development of the pacifist resistance movement of the prophets Tohu Kākahi and Te Whiti o Rongomai and the migration of Ngā Paerangi people in the 1870s to Parihaka, about 140 kilometres distant, to support the teachings of these prophets. Following their return to Kaiwhāiki in 1882, as outlined in Chapter 1, it was decided that Ngā Paerangi people and buildings would no longer be embellished with their history (tattoo and carvings), but they would rather look to the future through their children, and their histories and traditions would be maintained by the people. While recent research for Waitangi Tribunal Claims has triggered renewed interest in extant historical sources and the oral histories of community members, it is acknowledged that these histories were not always maintained. One con-sequence is that Charles Smith and the individual taonga collected by him no longer exist in iwi narratives.

Members of Ngā Paerangi recognise that knowledge has been lost. K. Clarke (personal communication, 26 July 2013) suggested this was a consequence of a number of factors including no one to pass information on to, or no need to pass information on, or no request for the knowledge, or the assumption that someone else would do it. Ngā Paerangi informants also believed their ancestors did not want their descendants to have this responsibility for this tangible heritage and its associated intangible qualities. Several reasons were given for this, including the belief that they did not have the skills to keep this heritage safe, and that forgoing traditional practices would make it easier to assimilate to Pākehā ways. Taonga were also given up for a range of reasons such as strengthening relationships or financial recompense. Simon (personal communication, 20 March 2013) articulated the importance of taonga as mechanisms for transmitting knowledge, while recognising that reading a carving, for example, is a skill that has been lost for most people today. Ngā Paerangi, therefore, have lost much through the processes of assimilation and colonisation, but they remain optimistic that opportunities will present themselves to recover what is needed when the time is right as these assemblages continue to form and reform.

Here and now . . .

This research also describes events that have emerged in the early twenty-first century as a consequence of developments in online access to museum collections, the effect of which has been to inspire new events. Significantly, the direct reconnection of Ngā Paerangi people with the taonga in 2013 when the group from Kaiwhāiki visited the Pitt Rivers Museum, was one such event. As Salmond (1984, p. 120) so elegantly expressed, "the alchemy of taonga was to bring about a fusion of [people] and ancestors and a collapse of distance in space-time."

I was able to identify a number of distinctive differences between New Zealand museums and those in England with regard to relationships with originating communities which are summarised in Table 3.1. I suggest that these differences result from the immediacy of Māori communities and New Zealand museums and the consequent impact of Māori representation and autonomy on museum practice over the past three decades, circumstances which have led naturally to what might be described as more effective collaborative practice in New Zealand.

Museums in New Zealand are involved with Waitangi Tribunal processes and aspirations for tribal development in ways that are not comparable to international museums in their own environments, even when post-colonial restitution and redress are taken into account. In the post-Treaty settlement environment, museum and individual responses to Treaty outcomes are

Table 3.1 Some differences between museum practice in New Zealand and England in relation to taonga Māori collections.

Closeness empowers by	Distance constrains by
Initiating collaborative practice with communities from outset	Inviting community participation once project defined and resourced
Supporting iwi (whānau/hapū) projects	Supporting museum projects
Immediacy in time and space	Delay
Face-to-face/personal	Anonymous/formal
Morally responsive	Institutionally/policy constrained
Classifications and descriptions based upon indigenous standards (Loza & Quispe, 2009)	Classifications based upon Western definitions of time and place, and visual analysis
Active and ongoing participation	Intermittent contact

evolving as a result of interactions and experiences whereby significant taonga are returning home. The effect of the Treaty of Waitangi today is about an *enduring* relationship, with principles of partnership, active protection and redress resulting from the Tribunal process. Of significance to museums in New Zealand is the legislation relating to moveable cultural property that sits within these principles.[1] Settlements resulting from the Tribunal processes have resulted in programmes of work for some tribal groups which may involve museums. Manatū Taonga Ministry for Culture and Heritage currently has more than 50 protocols with iwi and this number will increase (Manatū Taonga Ministry for Culture and Heritage, 2017, p. 20). Furthermore, there are significant repatriation claims involving Treaty breaches, such as the current negotiations with Rongowhakaata iwi relating to the return of Te Hau ki Tūranga wharenui from Te Papa to Gisborne, as well as resources dedicated to the Crown's commitment to reparation. Such claims have prompted Rhonda Paku (personal communication, 23 March 2014), previously senior curator mātauranga Māori at Te Papa, to caution that museum staff need to know their collections well so that they are able to respond to enquiries about collection holdings resulting from these processes. She also notes that letters of commitment and relationship agreements are some of the tools Te Papa is developing with iwi, as memoranda of understanding are no longer enough. Written agreements have replaced verbal agreements to guarantee perpetuity. Tribal groups enthusiastically embrace these processes. They are comfortable initiating these agreements as they have structures in place, in terms of authority and resources, as well as the confidence to negotiate outcomes desired by them. This is an important consideration for museums elsewhere as the heritage collections in their care become available online, and face-to-face interactions with originating communities become more commonplace.

As discussed in the introduction, over the past several decades museum practice has significantly changed as it affects communities (particularly indigenous groups) and their heritage. Schorch and Hakiwai (2014) succinctly summarise the causes of these changes in New Zealand museums, with identity politics manifest in development of methodologies, such as kaupapa Māori[2] employed in this study, and the legacy of *Te Māori*, which revealed the living relationship between taonga and communities of origin. New Zealand's national museum Te Papa has led local museum development following the *Museum of New Zealand Act 1992*. This Act has created a structure that embraces bicultural leadership and recognises kaitiakitanga and ownership of taonga by communities of origin, with a philosophy informed by the Mana Taonga principle which, through recognition of genealogical relationships with taonga, "gives iwi the right to care for their taonga, to speak about them, and to determine their use by the Museum" (Te Papa, 2015). Furthermore, an important aspiration of the staff who care for the taonga collection at Te Papa is the reconnection of people and their tribal taonga (ibid.). This museum has established a number of strategies for working with tribal communities to embed the Mana Taonga principle into museum practice, including a major exhibition programme in which design and development are collaborative and tribal elders are employed in residence at the museum. These strategies are useful models for (well-resourced) museums elsewhere. The experiences empower tribal communities to investigate collection holdings at museums, and outcomes of Tribunal inquiries are providing resources to negotiate cultural redress. As a result, taonga in museums are moving from little known and inaccessible to relevant and immediate.

Encounters of the type described earlier where Pēina was provided with an opportunity to hold and have her photograph taken with the taiaha of her ancestors, are a regular occurrence in museums that care for indigenous collections on an everyday operational basis. Museum staff in these increasingly common situations become familiar with the requirements of visitors during these encounters; a quiet space, time to come to terms with the experience of reconnection with their ancestral treasure and share the experience with each other, time to reflect, and usually the desire to touch or hold the item. In my experience, these opportunities are taken very seriously by Māori groups involved; individuals often bring a support person or group, including an individual able to take care of the spiritual aspects of the encounter, and they may travel a considerable distance for an opportunity to meet their ancestors (for the present case study community 19,000 kilometres). In New Zealand, for groups travelling from elsewhere in the country, appropriate manaakitanga by the host institution (involving an informal ceremonial welcome at the very least, and food, etcetera) is normal practice. If the staff of an institution do not have the required skills for these events, they are sought from the community. This requires good relationships with the local Māori communities and the ability to call on individuals from these communities, often at short notice, to facilitate these visits.

I have argued here that in New Zealand many museum practitioners work very much in the 'here and now' with Māori communities who are very immediate and present and vocal, rather than "over there and back then" in the context of Thomas' (2010) reference to indigenous people when museums work at distance from them. However, I acknowledge that while New Zealand museums are becoming more experienced with these activities, actions are dependent upon institutional and staff commitment and resourcing, are not universally practiced in New Zealand, are still evolving and have certainly not yet reached a stage of development that might be regarded as acceptable by Māori communities. Furthermore, such evolving procedures are also becoming embedded in museum practice elsewhere. For example, the Museum of World Cultures in Gothenburg, Sweden, has achieved important work regarding social inclusivity and indigenous viewpoints even when they are 'over there' (Muñoz, 2009). One conclusion I have drawn from this experience is that all such projects are driven by personalities who have become 'decolonial' (Mignolo, 2011) through their work and life experiences and are able to accept the validity of different knowledge systems and develop the means by which these can be articulated within the institution. However, personalities are transitory in the life of a museum object, and a decolonial position, while embedded in the individual, may not be embedded in the institution. An alternative is Lynch and Alberti's (2010) call for a more radical trust to democratise museum processes.

In this section I have discussed how one component of an assemblage, an historical collection, can move between assemblages and contribute to building relationships between them. Documenting the dynamic interactions of assemblage components over time and space provided the means by which their differences could be better understood. I have discussed the importance of historical collections as resources from the past influencing the present to inform the future and how this is epitomised through taonga in New Zealand museums, which can collapse distance in space-time. I have also acknowledged the validity of Māori concepts of space and time as central to a decolonised position with regard to curatorial responsibility in New Zealand. In addition I have discussed some of the distinctive differences between museum practices in New Zealand and other countries with regard to museum–indigenous community relationships, with the proximity of museums and communities resulting in the development of solutions for indigenous engagement and empowerment effective to varying degrees. Museums are becoming experienced facilitators of indigenous reconnection with heritage items but continuity of practice is also dependent upon individual and institutional commitment, which may be transitory. Finally, outcomes of the Treaty of Waitangi processes have potential implications for Ngā Paerangi's ongoing involvement with the Pitt Rivers Museum, but experience in Oxford has inspired a commitment to a relationship with this museum through these taonga.

Power

The second theme that has emerged from this research concerns the ways in which power is manifest within relationships. Differences can arise from epistemological and physical distance between indigenous communities and museums or conversely can be used to overcome them. Lynch (2011a, p. 148) considers the three different dimensions of power, distinguished by political and social theorist Stephen Luke, as the ability to get one's way despite resistance, to keep issues off the agenda and shape "the public domain through beliefs, values and wants" that are considered normal, and the way in which the powerless internalise and accept their condition. Whereas, Harris and O'Hanlon (2013, p. 10) intimate the positive benefits that are resulting from a shift in thinking in the way power is distributed within museum networks. This they suggest has been achieved through facilitating interactions between museums and originating communities, creating easier access to collections, and increased sensitivity when seeking information about museum objects from these communities. With specific reference to the case study, I will discuss how power, here delineated as authority and control, ability and privilege explicitly articulated through community and institutional priorities and resources, affects the ways in which museums and indigenous communities interact.

Authority and control

In the context of power in relation to social inclusion, as previously defined by Lynch, authority refers to the right to be in control and make decisions. Much work on museums and communities in settler societies has been undertaken with reference to the concept of the contact zone (Clifford, 1997) to explore the nature of relationships between indigenous peoples and others. Boast has criticised this model as neo-colonial and asymmetrical with museums remaining the "gatekeepers of authority and expert accounts" (Boast, 2011, p. 67). He suggests the complete redrafting of museum structures is required through which they "learn to let go of resources, even at times their objects, for the benefit and use of communities and agendas far beyond [their] knowledge and control" (ibid.). Even then Boast doubts this will result in a "perfect contact zone . . . of equal reciprocity and mutual benefit" (ibid., p. 63), equating it to a "a consultation that is designed from the outset to appropriate the resources necessary for the academy and to be silent about those that were not necessary" (ibid., p. 66), with the only results being to trap participants in documentation. Will this be the only outcome for Ngā Paerangi from their experience at the Pitt Rivers Museum: staff documentation of their week at the museum, augmented catalogue records, and any academic publications that may result?

The Pitt Rivers Museum's recent collaborations with Haida initially developed within the contact zone model. As the relationship between the institutional participants and Haida community members grew, however, through shared experiences at Oxford, new perspectives developed for some of the museum participants which Krmpotich and Peers (2013) refer to using the concept of the 'third space' where the repatriation of knowledge brought back into play by Haida members takes place (ibid., p. 191). This concept has also been used by Schorch and Hakiwai (2014) who have argued that this third space of knowledge production is created through a dialogue between indigenous practice and Western theory, centred on collaboration.

This positive outcome is aptly tempered by Clifford (2010) in his discussion of the meaning of the terms 'curator' and 'curate' when he concludes that, for the outsider, indigenous histories, which are non-linear and pragmatic in their orientation, will always be partially lost in translation. More recently, Harrison (2013, p. 6) proposed moving beyond the contact zone model through the exploration of synergies between curatorial and indigenous practices relating to 'custodial obligations.' This, he suggests, will lead to new ways of respectfully curating collections for today and into the future, from which new models will emerge through understanding the networks of material and social interactions with them (ibid., p. 5). Yet, his central premise, that indigenous practices are *equal* to museum curatorial expertise, nevertheless maintains the power and authority of the museum through determining and controlling these interactions.

By contrast, curator Adriana Muñoz's practice, developed through her work with indigenous communities at the Museum of World Cultures in Gothenburg, validates the synergies which occur when curatorial and indigenous practices meet. This is achieved through the respectful acknowledgement of different systems of knowledge, with neither superseding nor replacing the other (Muñoz, 2009). Concurring with the previous authors, she advocates practising "a democratic construction of knowledge" (ibid., p. 14) using a model that can be adopted elsewhere. In addition, Lynch (2014, p. 12) argues for the employment of a critical pedagogy within museums' public interface and urges open reflective practice for meaningful community engagement. Indigenous curating may be the only equitable solution for appropriate curation of indigenous collections. I argue, however, that such a solution is unlikely outside the home locale of indigenous peoples because indigenous curators require support – including appropriate policy, adequate resources, institution-wide responsiveness, and indigenous support networks – to address what Qureshi (2011, p. 87) describes as the "ideological weight of occupying such a privileged position." Furthermore, as Tapsell (2011, pp. 86–87) questions, is "*office* (ownership; museum values) willing to accommodate *kinship* (belonging; indigenous values) so each may co-exist and complement one another within museums"?

Numerous authors have examined the changes that have occurred in Western museums' practice over the past three decades in regard to indigenous collections and relationships with originating communities (for example, Boast, 2011; Kreps, 2011; Peers & Brown, 2003), describing the growing recognition of ethical responsibilities and commitment to change. Strategies for protecting indigenous knowledge systems are similarly recognised by a number of authors (for example, Battiste, 2008; Bishop, 2008). In these cases authority and outcomes favour indigenous communities (such as kaupapa Māori methodology) and self-determination is paramount.

This paradigm shift in Western museological thought and practice, in regard to authority over management, use and interpretation of indigenous heritage collections, has been highly visible at Te Papa with its adoption of a bicultural organisational structure, as discussed previously. This institution has moved beyond the collaborative model, viewed by some communities as "just alternative words for cultural appropriation and forms of neo-colonialism" (Kreps, 2011, p. 81), to one of more genuine partnership embodied within its bicultural leadership and practice.[3] This institution, particularly through its Māori and Pacific collections and community engagement, has embraced curatorial responsibility involving, as Clifford (2010, p. 7) has suggests, "active relations of reciprocity and dialogue – not administration or tutelage."

Elsewhere, other solutions have been tested. Ames (1999) describes exhibition development at the Canadian Museum of Anthropology between 1994 and 1996 involving First Nations' materials, which resulted in recognition of the need to change from cursory involvement by First Nations to full participation and the practices that evolved from that. This process acknowledged that to challenge "scholarly privilege is not necessarily a challenge to [its] value," but rather challenges who controls its 'direction and use' (ibid., p. 45). Despite the redistribution of institutional authority that followed, with traditional owners being able to affect control over exhibition outcomes (ibid., p. 49), he (citing Clifford, 1997, p. 207) warns "the solution is inevitably contingent and political." Muñoz (2009) also found this with her institution's work with Bolivian communities, which moved from collaborations between the museum and community specialists, to negotiations between their respective governments. This fear of a loss of control is what Lynch (2011a, p. 149) considers "the central undermining flaw within well-meaning attempts at democratizing museums." Furthermore, museums are constrained by their constitutions and funding sources and may even need to "conform to politicized directives" (Harris & O'Hanlon, 2013, p. 12). Finding creative solutions is necessary, without which collaborative partnerships will maintain their asymmetry.

Hence Boast's (2011, p. 64) suggestion that the new museology "promotes education over research, engagement over doctrine, and multivocality over connoisseurship" and is neoliberal through the open exchange of and access to information. Ethnographic museums in Europe and the United Kingdom, such as the Pitt Rivers Museum, have certainly expended considerable resources over the past decade to achieve open access to collection information via their online collection databases and expansion of their education, exhibition and events programmes, but do they otherwise fulfil Boast's definition of the new museology? As he reminds us, there is an asymmetry of knowledge transfer in the contact zone model; although both sides are egocentric, for the museum the transfer of knowledge is only one-way whereas for indigenous communities it is two-way.

Museums also have stewardship responsibilities and accountability beyond storing and interpreting if they are not to be perceived as "asymmetrical zones of appropriation" (ibid., p. 63). Indigenous responses to museums, as Erikson et al. (2002, p. 33) point out, have been visible through protests about the collecting and use of human remains, employment of indigenous staff, indigenous representation, and pressuring for repatriation of cultural patrimony. For these reasons Onciul (2011) developed the engagement zone model to counter this, while Krmpotich and Peers (2013, p. 52) described a 'third space' mentioned above.

Where do I, therefore, position the present research outcomes, which not only involve the repatriation of knowledge but also the generation of new knowledge based upon a critical analysis of the manifestations of power and divergent epistemologies? The values of respect and empathy are central to an appropriate contemporary museology to ensure that a more democratic construction of knowledge and distribution of power will result. To achieve this, collections need to be re-energised through our interactions with them and curators and interpreters must face up to and facilitate discussion about our difficult histories, including the ways in which collections have been acquired. As Mignolo asserts for ethnographic museums, the role of these institutions is not to show the visitor the beauty of a culture but rather what Western colonisation did to it (Sandahl & Mignolo, 22 May 2013).

At the outset of the encounter between the Pitt Rivers Museum and Ngā Paerangi in 2013, Ngā Paerangi had an expectation that one tangible result would be in the form of a jointly developed, museum-iwi agreement specifying the nature of their relationship and its potential future manifestations 'in perpetuity.' Staff however were unwilling to be a part of any formal signed agreement. This was reportedly to ensure that communication with a community was not restricted by particular signatories on a document, but rather that a more flexible and stronger relationship would be based upon establishing contacts with a number of people in a community. This informal relationship stands in marked contrast to the experience in New Zealand museums where tribal Māori expect an institutional partnership based around their heritage to centre upon an agreed and formalised document.

The reason for the reluctance to develop a formal agreement appears to be centred on concerns about the appropriateness of the signatory as a representative of the community who would control access to the collection in the future. Museum staff were unwilling to develop agreements where community power struggles, for example, might prevent access. Although perhaps understandable in a British or European context where relationships between ancient collections and contemporary descendants are disputed, it is a surprising response from a New Zealand perspective, where the value of established, mandated tribal leadership and management structures, for example, are recognised. In New Zealand museums these operate successfully and negotiated letters of agreement are common practice between organisations and Māori kin groups where the responsibilities and obligations of each party are clearly spelt out and agreed and there is no room for misunderstanding. I acknowledge that proximity in New Zealand has influenced the progressiveness of these developments, and that these processes will continue to be refined.

With regard to formal agreements, Coote (personal communication, 15 November 2013), with some justification, considers relationships between people are more effective than pieces of paper, but this is dependent upon the maintenance of these relationships and entails investment of time. As previously pointed out, he had a pragmatic point of view of museum-community relations over time with "perpetuity embedded in the objects" and any relationships reliant upon projects to carry them forward and keep them active. There was of course a constant demand on museum resources to engage in projects. Therefore, when the size and nature of the Pitt Rivers Museum collection is taken into account, as well as the staff resources and opportunities, the reality of their position on ongoing relationships with individual indigenous groups could be considered reasonable.

There was consensus among Ngā Paerangi members on possible outcomes from the museum visit: first and foremost they needed to fulfil manaaki (showing respect) responsibilities of descendants to acknowledge the mana (prestige and authority) of their ancestors through visiting the taonga in England; secondly, it was of utmost importance to assist museum staff to learn how to care for their taonga appropriately, to ensure the safety of the taonga as well as those people who came into contact with them; a third outcome was the potential for a visit home by the taonga, to open up educational opportunities around them deliverable through schools, museums and wānanga (educational seminars); accessibility of the collection and information about it digitally via the web was also important. Museum staff, on the other hand, felt it was important to enhance the collection documentation and identify how the taonga had been transferred between tribal community members and the collector. Accessibility of the taonga and the information they held about them to the people from whom the items originated was also important. Thus, while other network agents may have different requirements, expectations around the nature and potential outcomes of a contemporary relationship are not dissimilar for the indigenous and institutional components of this assemblage, although the former preferred a formalised approach specifying the nature of the relationship and its potential future manifestations, while the latter preferred a more informal arrangement.

In relation to the importance of an ancestral object within this network, there were, however, divergent positions. To briefly reiterate, for Māori people taonga are instantiations of ancestors, living embodiments of whakapapa (genealogy), whereas for "a university museum, a prime criterion for importance has to be [the object's] potential for research" (ibid.) and other museum programmes (education, exhibitions, events). There was also a perception of similarity in the museum use of ethnographic collections with Māori ideas about the animacy and the increasing mana of objects as they pass from one 'owner' to another.

Central to Coote's view is that he sees it as his responsibility to "unpick and unpack the past of objects in the collection . . . [then] by putting the collections out there, by publishing them, by exhibiting them, by putting them on the internet, etcetera, etcetera it becomes possible for them to be properly connected to the past" (ibid.). The emphasis here is on the exploration of historical data to unpack collections, a method that has been successfully applied for the present study. This certainly has benefits in that this is what Māori kin groups themselves are doing in order to recover lost histories. George Nuku's narrative on the tatā in the Pitt Rivers Museum collection and its meaning to him (discussed in Chapter 2) illustrate the potential of this. A useful approach, therefore, is to co-ordinate these methods with potential for enhancing results, as this study has demonstrated. It is also useful to take advantage of the fact that more and more people have double knowledge systems and can unpack the cultural context of objects in ethnographic collections and thus greatly enhance their academic and museological value, if they are given the opportunity.

While acknowledging that it is best to leave questions of meaning, significance and symbolism to specialists, as Coote suggests, it would be useful to work in partnership with these specialists to make these meanings as accessible to others as institutional and academic publications are accessible. This would be immensely valuable, as many indigenous experts visit the museum to work with staff and collections. Joint publications from this research or distribution of this knowledge in other ways would be a significant contribution to this field.

Ability

Ability is the second manifestation of power visible from the analysis of results. It is characterised here by the knowledge, skills and experiences brought to this study by participants to progress specific planned outcomes. Recognising that museum staff and Ngā Paerangi people who travelled to Oxford had very different experiences and skills in relation to museums and museum collections, each group attempted to anticipate how best to use and share their respective skills and knowledge for mutual benefit during their brief time together. Both groups exhibited some degree of anxiety about fulfilling the expectations of the other. Staff were able to address this through detailed planning for the visit: the welcome, allocated responsibilities for staff, and insight into Ngā Paerangi expectations for the week. Similarly, the Ngā Paerangi group met regularly before travel to plan their approach, discuss opportunities that might arise, identify and delegate responsibilities and requirements for the visit, practice waiata for ceremonial occasions, communicate with other tribal members, and so forth.

The Ngā Paerangi group shared responsibilities to achieve set aims, reflecting individual knowledge and skills. For example, one informant, Ngā Paerangi leader Simon, repeatedly deferred to his nephew Rzoska, the acknowledged tribal genealogy expert, when discussing the identification of people in photographs, as this was the role that Rzoska had been chosen for and the knowledge that he had developed far surpassed that of his uncle.

The museum staff's prior experience working with indigenous communities ensured sensitivity to the potential requirements of the Ngā Paerangi group. The strategy for receiving and hosting them took this into account and the museum was genuine about developing appropriate methods to deal with new situations. They also documented their experience of the visit in detail to add to the collection records so as to provide a permanent record for the institution. This strategy had been successfully implemented for a previous visit by a Haida delegation, so the visit was "recorded in terms of an anthropological study of what happens when a group visits a European museum full of their own material culture. Also note taking to inform the database as to how objects are actually used and how they may have been made" (Belsey, personal communication, 12 November 2013). Furthermore, the Ngā Paerangi group acknowledged that the museum and its skilled staff were responsible for the preservation of a significant proportion of their extant tangible heritage, from which they now had the opportunity to rebuild cultural capital in the form of associated intangible heritage, kinship networks, education resources and more.

An important finding of this study is the identification of the difficulties of genuine engagement with communities in practice. I observed opportunities that arose during this project which, despite everyone's best efforts, were curtailed because of the constraints imposed by a three-year doctoral research programme. These restraints included availability of individuals to participate, time constraints, and the limited experience of some of the group with museums and academia, thereby constraining outcomes.

An active rather than a passive approach to museum–iwi interactions would have resulted in more control of the encounter with the museum and insistence on a formal agreement between them, acquiescence to opportunities for information dissemination while maintaining control over this knowledge, and encouraging the museum to take the project further and at least share if not take responsibility for seeking fiscal partners to facilitate it. However, it is useful to be reminded of the responsibilities of tribal accountability, and that time would enable further outcomes to eventuate for both parties.

Privilege

Privilege is the final manifestation of power falling out of this assemblage, considered here in terms of community and institutional priorities, opportunities and access to resources. While acknowledging that privilege is contextual, Lynch (2011a, p. 149) observed, through self-reflexive practice within her own institution, that even well-meaning museum staff, aware that their own position was a result of privilege "somehow appeared to feel that this awareness exempted them from its consequences." But firstly, returning to two of the historical components of this assemblage and their interactions, I consider the opportunities that arose from the status of two key actors, Charles Smith and Te Oti Takarangi.

Takarangi was the leader of one of the largest tribal groups on the Whanganui River during the nineteenth century and controlled a sizeable and strategic location near the fledgling settler town and port of Whanganui, with the defensive, resource and alliance benefits these factors afforded. Of particular relevance to this study is the mutually beneficial relationship he established with Charles Smith, his 'Pākehā' with the advantages and responsibilities this entailed, while Te Oti Takarangi was Smith's source of labour, security, tribal information and material goods.

At the same time, Smith's privileged position within the European society provided him with respect and acceptance in a settler community, time and opportunity to pursue a range of interests, as well as time and resources to travel regularly and extensively. Various influences, both before he emigrated from England and after his arrival in Whanganui, enabled his collection to develop. Moreover, the volume of material in both the Pitt Rivers and Whanganui Regional Museum collections originating from Charles Smith indicates that he made the most of opportunities to acquire items, being aware of the increasing scarcity of material for collecting and making every endeavour to obtain items where he could.[4] He was also a ready source of the material goods Ngā Paerangi people were eager to acquire and for which, in some cases, they chose to part with items that they were aware Smith had an interest in. The pāoi (flax pounder) in the collection sold to Smith by Tutaria is an example of this.

In contrast, travel today across half the globe to visit the taonga of their ancestors was a massive financial undertaking for Ngā Paerangi members, as well as an emotional, spiritual and organisational one; for some it is never to be repeated, while for many others it will remain an unattainable experience. A focus on whānau and marae often takes precedence over travel outside New Zealand, while for those with family living overseas, visiting them is a priority over travel for any other reason.

Pitt Rivers Museum staff make every effort to accommodate indigenous groups once contact is established. The effect of some museum practices on communities of origin, however, may not always be a positive one. Although this is not the museum's intention, the impact of advances in online access to collections of significance to indigenous communities is that they want direct access, if not to the items themselves, then to the staff responsible for caring for these items. This project identified the challenges a small staff at a major institution with an international reputation face, responding to the volume of requests they receive. Observing Macdonald's (2002) criticism that museum staff often are too object-focused, describing this as "the fetishization of material culture," Byrne (2013, pp. 221–223) suggested "that paying closer attention to the social practices of which objects once were a part and the relationship between objects in practices when carrying out collection research has the potential to create longer lasting, more embedded collaboration." This is the nature of museum practice in many New Zealand museums and one which I promote in my professional practice as a curator, researcher and teacher. However, one of the issues that emerged from the findings of this study is that institutions responsible for world culture collections and physically remote from the communities of origin have to balance all requests for time and resources and do not necessarily prioritise indigenous groups over other research enquirers.

Central to ethical museum practice in the twenty-first century is the responsibility for making collections and their documentation accessible. I acknowledge that resource limitations impact on museum responsiveness to collection accessibility, and that this is not an issue restricted to the Pitt Rivers Museum. Responsiveness to requests for access to indigenous heritage in New Zealand and elsewhere, however, has resulted in the development of innovative practices centred upon recognition of indigenous authority over cultural heritage, as well as formal and informal procedures to control access. Much can be gained by museum staff accommodating indigenous cultural practices through inverting power relations and the voice of authority as Kreps (2011, p. 75) recommends. Releasing power to make decisions about the management of and access to collections to those who would benefit most directly from this has also been shown to have two-way benefits, to the institution as well as to the community. However, this brings into play the responsibilities of the institution to their own diverse communities (for the case study those in and around Oxford), including the research community who rely upon the museum's collection for their own benefits, and the impact of the political environment and funding sources. This is, however, where differences in institutional practices in England, and in countries with indigenous communities close at hand are most clear. In New Zealand museums for example, there are numerous examples of the evolution of staff and governance structures and policy development which mirror the changes that are taking place in society, where the devolution of power to all stakeholders enables more equitable processes and relationships.

The resources available today to the museum and iwi identified by this research that relate to the distribution of power are tabulated in Table 3.2. As Paku (personal communication, 23 March 2014) reminds us, "We are paid to do our jobs, iwi aren't." It is important to remember that they have other priorities as well. For Ngā Paerangi these priorities relate to whānau first and foremost, and their health, education, employment, housing as well as marae sustainability and capital developments. Because of current resource (time and people) constraints, the response to the opportunity in Oxford was not as effective as it might have been at a different time. Correspondingly,

Table 3.2 Comparing resources between Ngā Paerangi iwi and Pitt Rivers Museum.

Ngā Paerangi Resources	*Pitt Rivers Museum Resources*
Time limited	Staff and time limited
Intangible heritage rich	Tangible heritage (collection and documentation) rich
Personal community (whānau, hapū and iwi) focussed	Professional community (institution and academy) focussed
Marae	Institution – museum and university
Tribal networks	Professional – museum and academic – networks
Personal reputation	Professional reputation
Indigenous focus on collective responsibility	Western focus on individual rights and advancement
Skills in customary practices	Collection care skills and resources
Knowledgeable about tribal histories and genealogies, customary practices	Research skills and academic specialty knowledge rich
Fiscal limited	Funding potential

Coote recommended considerable advance notice of the Ngā Paerangi visit to Oxford because of the busy schedule of institution staff (personal communication, 10 May 2012).

Owing to the paucity of extant Ngā Paerangi taonga in the Whanganui museum, this tribal community is in general inexperienced in dealing with museums and had no expectation that taonga originating from their community would be held in a museum. Today Ngā Paerangi's strengths are, in the first instance, whānau, hapū and iwi and, in the context of this study, represented by intangible forms of heritage including te reo Māori (language), tāhuhu kōrero (history) and tikanga (customary values and practices). Furthermore and significantly, they are one of the few iwi to have, over time, retained a sizeable population at their home marae. Conversely, while the museum relies upon subject specialists, historical documentation, and more recently indigenous knowledge holders to contextualise material in their care, the institution is rich in collection and research skills, enjoys the opportunities provided by Oxford University status, and has benefitted from recent architectural refurbishments.

As previously stated, for Māori people, tribal accountability is central to tribal decision-making and focusses resources on community requirements, specifically within whānau, hapū and iwi. Within Western ontologies, however, a clear demarcation is usually made between personal and professional. For the case study assemblage, the museum staff's priorities clearly focussed around their institutional responsibilities in the first instance, with the museum collection at the centre of this, whereas for tribal kin, value was placed upon the relationships between the taonga and people.

This research documents the limitations and issues generated from differences in resources available to components within this relational assemblage, as well as activities prioritised. As well the lack of overlap between Ngā Paerangi perceptions of the nature of relationships between them today (they are continuing the relationship that existed between their ancestors and the recipients of the taonga gifts, with the current custodians of the taonga) and staff perceptions that a personal response, beyond that initiated by Ngā Paerangi, is currently outside their abilities and resources. Outcomes in terms of relationships built may therefore stall when the current project ends, as Peers and Brown (2003, p. 9) observe,

> Though many relationships begin with a specific project . . . community expectations are that such projects are vehicles to developing long-term relationships, while museums may assume their responsibilities are over when the project ends.

From this discussion it is clear that privilege, in terms of community and institutional priorities, opportunities and access to resources varies throughout this assemblage. Historically, mutually beneficial outcomes resulted. Today epistemological and physical distance between the network components as well as resource limitations and external demands impact on responsiveness to opportunities the encounters between them may generate.

In this section I have discussed how power, delineated as authority, control, ability and privilege, is manifest within and between the assemblage components and the effect of this on the ways in which museum and indigenous networks interact. I identified that recognition of power within these interactions can democratise knowledge production in the indigene–museum network with the approach utilised by the present study providing opportunity for advancing a decolonised museum practice. As Sully (2007, p. 222) states, a decolonised position "offers a means of addressing the asymmetrical interconnectivity that entwines the lives of the coloniser and colonised." To enable the voices of the colonised to be heard requires involving them in the conversation from the beginning, respecting their points of view, letting go of control, empowering through sharing resources, as well as utilising institutional skills and resources to initiate projects prioritised by them.

I have also shown in this section that bringing together the range of skill sets that have emerged from this network indicates the creative and generative potential of the heritage network. Finally, discussion has centred on the distance between network components. Although it may not be possible to reduce physical distance, respectful acknowledgement of the epistemological distance may enable responsiveness to opportunities where differential access to resources is countered by a willingness to work towards a common purpose. Lynch (2011a, p. 155) states that it is better to "be understood as the political space of encounter between adversaries, where the power relations which structure these encounters are brought to the fore [as this] creates a liberating effect for museums and their community partners." Peers and Brown (2003, p. 2) share this view, commenting that this can "produce something of value for both parties." Although I agree with their statement that a museum's obligations to its publics, its governance structure and to the museum profession differ from those of communities of origin to their stakeholders (ibid., p. 8), indigenous communities of origin *are* one of the museum's publics, and obligations to governance and the profession are contingent and political, whereas cultural obligations transcend time and space.

Values

> Tōu piki amokura nōu, tōku piki amokura nōku. History must be viewed through both our lens.
>
> Office of Treaty Settlements (2014, p. 18)

The final theme to emerge from this research relates to values. Values are the ethical rules or principles by which we define ourselves and which guide our actions. In Prown's (1982, p. 3ff) view, values can be defined as intrinsic, utilitarian, aesthetic, spiritual, or the way in which they are expressed to others or the world. Taking these definitions into account in material culture studies enables us to circumvent our own cultural biases. The communities of interest in this study – indigenous owner, collector, academic, museum professional – have diverse value systems. Thinking through the differences between them is a key element of this study and one that aims to bridge cultural difference, which, as Clavir (2002) claims, is central to an appropriate museology in the twenty-first century.

Values important to Māori, all underpinned by tikanga, have been identified by Mead (2003, pp. 28–30): whanaungatanga embracing whakapapa and focusing on relationships; manaakitanga which is about nurturing relationships, looking after people; mana which relates to an individual's standing in a community; tapu; noa; utu which can be defined as compensation, revenge, reciprocity; and ea as the successful closing of a sequence, the restoration of relationships or satisfaction.

Commonalities and differences between Māori, New Zealander and European cultural values have been identified by Atkinson (2014, p. 76), from which she concludes that,

New Zealand cultural values can be seen in relation to the influences on, and development of, identity. Aotearoa New Zealand has now moved away from purely European cultural values and is more a mixture or blending, but also distortion, of European and Māori values.

Underlying epistemological and ontological frameworks, therefore, negate the ability to fit the values of the communities of interest in this study, into a universal value system.

A central premise of this research, however, is that taking into account underlying epistemological and ontological differences will improve understanding of the past and present life of taonga for the originating community and museum. As described previously, for Māori, as for many indigenous communities, a close relationship exists between people and things. Taonga are seen as living entities, the spiritual embodiment of ancestors and are central to Māori cultural identity. Conversely, although Western museum staff may have an anthropological appreciation of this view of an animate life force, and some major shifts in thinking have been achieved and documented respecting difference (Golding & Modest, 2013; Muñoz, 2009; Peers & Brown, 2003), a general perception of objects relates to their physical or aesthetic attributes, ability to provide historical or scientific data, and their illustrative or interpretative function in exhibitionary narratives. This is still very evident in our museums. Accordingly, the value systems of indigenous and many museum communities are significantly different and, in consequence, so are the ways in which objects in museums are regarded. Discussion of these differences is the focus of this section.

Alternative value systems

Referring to research by Russo with the Native American tribe Lummi, Atkinson (2014, p. 59) states that "gaining insight into the world views of others did not allow for harmonization, but it did facilitate a respectful distance." Lynch (2011b, 2013) advocates socially responsible, open and collaborative reflective practice. For this Māori–English case study I will use whakapapa, the Māori philosophy of kinship, to illustrate this point.

Whakapapa is the central uniting force of Māori kin groups. When Māori people introduce themselves to each other, they identify their ancestral links to places and people and in this way establish the relationships between them, and where they position themselves. Whakapapa, as Tapsell (2011, p. 87) explains, is "more than vertical or horizontal memory lists of ancestors. It is the way by which tribal Māori systematically order themselves and their relationships to customary estates." Taonga also have whakapapa, which link people today with their past. As Peers and Brown (2003, p. 6) state, objects "prompt the transmission of cultural knowledge across generations" without which these stories might not have been told in the present.

One Ngā Paerangi taonga in the Pitt Rivers Museum, the hoeroa mentioned earlier, illustrates ancestry describing relationships forged. The hoeroa, Ngā Karu o Niu Tīreni, (see Chapter 1 and Figure 3.2) is an example of the potential of taonga for "collapsing generations of time" (Tapsell, 2011, p. 87) as it can illustrate Ngā Paerangi ancestors' support of the Kīngitanga in the nineteenth century outlined in Chapter 1. The 'giving up' of this taonga by Whanganui Māori following the taking of the Oath of Allegiance to the Crown was an immensely powerful act signifying the severing of their allegiance with the Māori King through passing the symbol of their support for the Kīngitanga to a representative of the British Government. Despite the magnitude of such events, without these memory triggers, the events and the relationships they represent become fainter over time until, as Rzoska and others have stated, they are ready to reveal themselves again. Ngā Karu o Niu Tīreni's recently rediscovered name illustrates this.[5]

An important additional point when considering indigenous community impetus for actions relates to "ancestral accountability, any actions in the present, need to remain in alignment with past generations' leadership decisions, while maintaining continuity into the future" (Tapsell, 2011, p. 87). These inherent requirements for accountability through time placed considerable pressure on Wīpaki Peeti, in particular, and the other members of the

Figure 3.2 Ngā Paerangi members, Michelle Horwood and museum staff viewing and discussing taonga including the hoeroa named Ngā Karu o Niu Tīreni, the long whalebone staff, alongside the taiaha Te Maungārongo, Te Oti Takarangi's tewhatewha, and Wiremu Pātene's tewhatewha, 2013.

Photo by Teresa Peeti.

Ngā Paerangi group while in Oxford. Peeti is the great grandson of Tāmati Takarangi and therefore the senior living relative of Tāmati and his uncle Te Oti Takarangi. The role of Peeti and his daughter Teresa Peeti in this project cannot be understated. By participating in the journey to Oxford they recognised and accepted the immense responsibilities placed upon them and responded accordingly.

As pointed out in Chapter 1, Te Oti Takarangi and others who made gifts to Charles Smith placed obligations upon him when they presented him with ancestral taonga. Although he may not have been fully aware of his reciprocal responsibilities regarding these gifts, his relationship with members of Ngā Paerangi was such that they maintained this relationship over five decades while he resided at Te Korito, and must therefore have been satisfied with the outcomes. The nature of Smith's relationships with members of Ngā Paerangi, as far as can be deduced from the research findings, in particular his relationship with Te Oti Takarangi, suggests one of mutual respect and benefit. One explanation for this is that Smith may have been informally adopted into Te Oti Takarangi's extended family, becoming Takarangi's 'Pākehā,' bound into tribal genealogical networks through his "acts of kindness and alliance" (Salmond, 2017, p. 145). Furthermore, he was comfortable visiting the marae at Kaiwhāiki and interacting with Ngā Paerangi people, and inviting them into his home. This was not a typical action among the settler community at that time, although there are other notable exceptions such as Anglican missionary Richard Taylor. As noted, Ngā Paerangi's overland route to Taranaki went through Smith's farm and this route remained open to them throughout the conflicts of the 1860s. Also, during this period of unrest, Te Oti Takarangi ensured Smith and his property remained unscathed as a result of any immediate conflict. The gifts Smith received clearly establish his mana within this community and his recognition of and respect for Māori values and their associated protocols, including whakapapa, manaakitanga and whanaungatanga.

So far this section has focussed on the commonalities and differences in values evident within and between the assemblage components. The following section will discuss these contextually for the case study communities.

Articulating the differences

Clavir (2002) employed a comparative methodology to articulate the differences between First Nations and museum perspectives on heritage and heritage items based upon belief systems. I have adopted this approach to outline differences in values between Ngā Paerangi/Māori and Pitt Rivers Museum/English museums relating to ethnographic collections, elicited from my research data; specifically interviews and observations, augmented with reference to theoretical and historical literature and my own professional experience as a museum curator. A summary of the results of this analysis is presented in Table 3.3.

From this it is possible to articulate some of the values that differentiate museums and Māori communities, whether they have changed over time, and the effect these differences have on their ability to work towards a common purpose (in terms of effecting a long-term and mutually beneficial relationship around the taonga). The findings also accord with earlier observations describing how heritage items are viewed in terms of their intrinsic value, function and agency by indigenous communities and museums.

Table 3.3 Differences in values within a relational network of a tribal Māori community and English museum and the effects of these differences on working towards a common purpose: A comparative approach (after Clavir, 2002).

Ngā Paerangi	*Pitt Rivers Museum*
Differences	
Taonga	Object
Tapu and animate	Respecting notions of animacy
Safeguarding people	Safeguarding objects
Safe-keeps	Collects, documents, cares for
Use, perform	Exhibit, research
Cultural ownership/kaitiakitanga	Legal ownership
Primary function is reaffirmation of tribal values and history; oral traditions; holistic/cyclic	Primary function is collect, document, research; Western intellectual traditions (science and social science); linear
Taonga connect the past to the present and future, contracting time	Objects are witnesses to the past, with value in the present
Māoricentric	Eurocentric
Keeping taonga warm (McKenzie, 1993)	Conserving, preserving
Returning to Papatūānuku (Earth Mother)	
Effects	
Relationships are about people	Relationships are embedded in the object
Taonga as opportunities for relationships (gift exchange)	Objects as opportunities for research funding and academic achievement
Tribal access to cultural knowledge	Public access to all knowledge
Home, marae	Museum
Personal	Institutional
Collective decision-making	Individual/Institutional decision-making
Exhibits by cultural group	Exhibits by form and function

"Look at the waka huia all by itself . . . feeling lonely without its partner." Teresa Peeti made this observation when she first encountered this taonga in the galleries at the Pitt Rivers Museum during the 2013 visit. Her response clearly illustrated the affective impact of encountering a taonga from home, with her empathy for the vessel's separation from its lid demonstrating the object's animacy in her world view. Along with her whanaunga she was awed by the museum displays, by the volume and the range of material available in one place, having experienced nothing quite like it before. Thus a further observation relates to the abundant scale of museum collection holdings, which can be difficult for indigenous communities to reconcile with the paucity of extant tangible heritage available to them in their home area, where they would be most useful to them today.

Another important observation of different viewpoints that has implications for museum practice relates to touching objects. Touching is a part of keeping taonga warm (McKenzie, 1993). Pitt Rivers Museum have constructively responded to this challenge to professional practice by putting strategies in place to facilitate such cultural requirements. The institution's perspective is that the positive outcomes outweigh any negative ones in these encounters.

The ability to use taonga is central to the continuity of the knowledge embedded within them. Access to museum collections by indigenous communities in post-settler nations has been fundamental in the revitalisation of some traditional practices, such as stone tool technology. However, some issues regarding access for practitioners can be in conflict with orthodox museum practices. The rejuvenation of taonga pūoro (Māori musical instruments) in New Zealand is an example of this, where museums face challenges dealing with requests to use the collections in their care. In some cases these requests have been turned into mutually beneficial opportunities with innovative solutions developed, such as the commissioning of new items to fulfil this practical role and authorisation of specialists to use the historical collection items. Āwhina Tamarapa, Te Papa's taonga Māori curator until 2016, is a member of a nation-wide group of taonga pūoro revivalists, Haumanu. She embeds her learning from involvement in this group within her work practice to support the restoration of technological practices and to develop new ways to make mātauranga Māori (Māori knowledge) accessible to museum publics.

Respecting world views different from one's own, as discussed in the introduction, "may involve conceiving objects in different ways, as living entities, some of which retain spiritual power sufficient to endanger workers and visitors alike" (Sully, 2007, p. 37). Museum practices have been evolving to address this. This can be illustrated at the Whanganui Regional Museum, where, until the mid-1980s, there was no physical demarcation between storage areas for human remains and other cultural material, so descendants visiting a taonga in storage may well have come face-to-face with one of their ancestors unexpectedly as well. Significant improvements in museum storage and display at the museum were achieved around this time including removal from display and separate storage from other collections for all human remains.

My first major contribution to the museum's recognition of its responsibilities to descendant communities was the removal to Te Papa of the one toi moko (preserved tattooed human head) in the collection, the display of which had been the root cause of a lot of the community ill feeling toward the museum. I also sought guidance from a Māori advisory group on ways in which the museum could address past practices that had affected the institution's credibility in some quarters. A series of tapu removal procedures was instigated for all spaces within the museum. Since then, the museum has embraced the constitutional reform described earlier and strategies have been effected to ensure the cultural safety of all visitors and staff. More recently, in 2017, reconfigured storerooms have enabled the physical and therefore culturally appropriate separation of groups of taonga.

These developments equate with those happening elsewhere that have embedded a decolonised museology into Western museum practice, in particular, increased autonomy in the management of indigenous heritage collections as a response to the democratisation of museum practice and enhanced community engagement (Lonetree, 2012; Onciul, 2015). Also, as McCall and Gray (2013) point out, the practical implementation of such a democratised position is linked to the values held by museum workers themselves and how they relate them to their professional practice. As stated in the introduction, the three museological themes for moral agency explored by Marstine (2011) include social inclusion, radical transparency and the shared guardianship of heritage. Kreps (2011) and Tapsell (2011) concurring with these themes, question whether museums are ready to decolonise through the inverting of power relations and the voice of authority.

This is a central argument of this study. By recognising and acknowledging differences in values, Ngā Paerangi and the Pitt Rivers Museum can develop a mutually beneficial relationship, but only if each is prepared to work towards a common purpose. For example, Hāwira has agreed to document for the museum staff cultural guidelines for Ngā Paerangi taonga to ensure the safety of taonga and staff. Staff have readily agreed to implement these within the constraints of museum professional practice and resources. Likewise, staff, since the 2013 visit, have explored at least one way to progress the inclusion of Māori knowledge during the development of a new display that includes taonga from the Charles Smith collection. A staff member approached one member of Ngā Paerangi to assist with the interpretation of this display. However, while the museum initiated dialogue with Ngā Paerangi over the type of interpretation they were proposing and whether it was factually correct, and asked for advice, they did not involve Ngā Paerangi at the outset but had already developed a conceptual plan for the display, selected the content and drafted the interpretative text. From an outside observer's perspective, it seems they were only requesting authority to sign off what they had determined as the most appropriate content for the display and they were asking an individual with no previous experience of museum interpretation or museum processes to advise on content. While this, perhaps, can be commended as a first step, involvement of tribal experts at the outset from the conceptual development on, while generating more work for staff, would also generate significant benefits for them and for visitors to the institution, including a depth of understanding in display interpretation not possible outside the tribal community.

Following from this, another factor arising from the reassembling of historical and contemporary components is ownership. On one hand, as mentioned in the introduction, this relates to an inalienable connection between people and things (Kramer, 2006), while on the other it is defined by the Western judicial system. Māori perspectives, which have changed little over time, relate to customary ownership and kaitiakitanga; whereas museum staff, while acknowledging difference, comply with the legal responsibilities of their governing bodies. Māori communities, although they may have lost legal ownership have never relinquished cultural ownership, which is manifest in New Zealand museums through the mana taonga and kaitiakitanga principles and philosophies. For museums in post-settler nation-states moral responsiveness has resulted from living in proximity to indigenous communities. Whanganui Regional Museum, for example, has also adopted and implemented repatriation policies (for taonga in 2008 as well as human remains in 2006).

Furthermore, taonga in New Zealand museums may have different legal status to that of museum objects elsewhere, as in certain circumstances museums there accept taonga as long-term loans rather than outright gifts. This is in response to Māori community members who require a place to keep taonga safe but who are unwilling to relinquish ownership. New Zealand museums recognise that kaitiaki responsibilities may be shared with descendants of taonga. For Western museums elsewhere ownership is legal and binding. In this study, individual Ngā Paerangi respondents had a range of perspectives on their ability to care for their taonga today; some recognised that they did not have adequate resources to care for their taonga physically at home, while others focussed more upon the spiritual and cultural wellbeing of the taonga and believed they could only be appropriately cared for in Whanganui and only by someone from Ngā Paerangi.

Numerous authors have considered ontological differences. Mignolo (2013, p. 1) for example, uses Nigerian writer Chimamanda Ngozi Adichie's celebrated speech "The danger of a single story" to illustrate how a story can obscure multiple world views,

> The power of a single story is that it can make us believe that the world is as the story tells it, without questioning the authors who are constructing the narrative. It is the kind of story that transcends the status of 'fictional narrative' and becomes ontology – or 'reality.'

Thus, once in the public domain, a single story can become a hegemonic truth. This constructed reality may therefore negate the role and value of an object for tribal identity and social, economic and cultural development within the originating culture. This issue was recently addressed by Hakiwai (2014), where he illustrates the importance of describing the place of objects within culture from an 'insider' tribal perspective. He was able to demonstrate that "taonga are symbols and icons of tribal identity that help to resolve and heal the brokenness and fractures of colonial experience" (ibid., p. 241). Mignolo (2009) has also regularly discussed ideas of relativism, which sees all explanations of the past as equally valid, with none able to replace another. When discussing the Kallawayan Niño Korin collection from Bolivia at the Museum of World Cultures in Gothenburg, Mignolo contended that to suggest one description is more reliable than another is to "misunderstand the problem. Both have the truth but in [a] different universe of discourse: [museum director] Wassén's description shall be debated by museums curators; Kallawaya's description shall be debated by other Kallawayas" (ibid., p. 5).

Opportunity for these divergent perspectives is not always possible in the Western museum public interface. For example, Coote (personal communication, 15 November 2013), while describing the nature of displays at the Pitt Rivers Museum as "about celebrating human creativity and ingenuity and putting all cultures on the same level of creativity and ingenuity and historicity", goes on to state that, at the same time, "one of the frustrations of the museum is that it doesn't lend itself to . . . really providing insights into other ways of seeing the world" (ibid.). This is achieved to some extent at this museum through short-term exhibitions, related events and indigenous community involvement in exhibition interpretation, as discussed earlier. Furthermore, as Sully (2007, p. 39), quoting Merriman (2000), states, "object meaning, rather than being inherent and singular is multiple and contingent, negotiated, and renegotiated as social contexts shift around them," thereby recognising that authenticity and meaning are negotiable and constructed; the past is constantly reconstructed in the present. Thus multiple ways of understanding the past are influenced by cultural as well as social and political contexts.

As the results of this study have shown, while Pitt Rivers Museum staff are guided by their personal ethics and philosophies, they are bound and led by institutional policies and practices, whereas tribal Māori, while also guided by their personal values, operate through a system of collective decision-making. The findings of the current research are consistent with those of Clavir (2002) indicating that the identification of differences as well as commonalities in value systems between indigenous people and museums, as well as methods to bridge the cultural distance between them, is central to an appropriate museology in the twenty-first century. From this I conclude that building on and applying this new knowledge about value systems will enhance the ability of museum staff to engage meaningfully with communities of origin. Likewise, Atkinson (2014, p. 75) writes that for museum professionals "ultimately, people need to put themselves in the position of having to learn, as this facilitates the identification of common points of understanding and misunderstanding."

Results from this study affirm that museums and indigenous people value relationships and that these must be two-way and actively maintained. Nonetheless, the museum position is that the relationship is embedded in the object. Museum staff place emphasis on this, whereas indigenous groups look to people to establish a relationship with and once this has happened will work together to develop opportunities that fall out of this relationship. Furthermore, because of resourcing demands, museums are realistic in identifying that the catalyst for and continuity of a relationship relies on a project.

Ngā Paerangi participants in this project were there to represent their whānau, hapū and iwi; responsibilities were therefore local, personal and genealogically related, and community-focussed. By contrast, participants from Pitt Rivers Museum, while drawing on a range of personal principles that influenced their actions, were employed by and spoke for their institution and embraced the professional values of the museum industry. This is entirely expected and natural. The implications of this, however, are that these groups are not necessarily dissimilar. They both, while maintaining a level of autonomy, must refer to their respective 'sponsor' for any major decision, and are reliant upon place-based approaches, which have their own distinctive and embedded value systems.

Harrison (2013, p. 12) notes that museums acknowledge different value systems, for example, by creating a category on databases where indigenous values are documented. Without negating the advances in museum practice where indigenous sensitivities are taken on board (such as restrictions for menstruating women), this does not necessitate reform of the system with "the original categories and underlying values on which they rest often remaining in place" (ibid.). This has resulted in indigenous exploration and adoption of alternative digital platforms and databases for knowledge management and sharing of cultural heritage (Horwood, 2017). However, this does not take into account the heritage that has been gathered up by and will remain in Western museums. Whereas, employing a comparative museology "for the development of more inclusive, cross-cultural approaches to cultural heritage management" advocated by Kreps (2003, p. 19), will liberate not only culture but also our view from a Western museological paradigm of what constitutes a museum, an object and museological practice so we are better able to 'recognise alternative forms' (ibid., p. 145).

It is apparent that communities must find ways to develop and employ strategies that continue to exercise their values in the museum at distance. This they can achieve by building relationships with the staff responsible for their cultural patrimony and guiding them in the care of this heritage to ensure the cultural safety not only of the objects but of the people they come into contact with, and by continuing to pursue these aims until mutually agreeable outcomes are reached. Moreover institutional staff have a moral responsibility as the transitory guardians of significant proportions of this cultural patrimony to safeguard it in culturally responsive ways and, as the single access point to this material for communities of origin or other institutional publics, to facilitate this access in appropriate ways, which may include face-to-face interactions.

In concluding this section, which has focussed upon the differences in values between Western collecting institutions and indigenous communities in relation to heritage objects, I refer to Clavir (2002, p. 121) who maintains that the "Western positivist meta-narrative is linear, scientific, isolates the parts to gain an understanding of the whole, and contends that the world benefits from universal access to knowledge" which contradicts indigenous narratives. I argue that this study, through disassembling the parts, however, allows for recognition of the relational networks of which they are a part. I have also demonstrated that indigenous assemblages form and reform as a result of interactions between their component parts. This reassembling is visible in Ngā Paerangi's re-engagement with their taonga at Oxford, and will be ongoing in potential future interactions between any and all of these components.

Conclusion

The three overriding themes that have emerged from analyses of the components of a heritage assemblage – a community, a museum, a heritage collection and collector – are the concepts of time and space, power and values, all of which contribute to a better understanding of how the nature of relationships between them could change. The first theme documented the dynamic interactions of these disassembled entities through time and space and provided the means by which their differences could be better understood. The second theme addressed the manner in which power, manifest as authority and control, ability and privilege, within and between assemblage components, affects the ways in which museums and indigenous communities interact. It is clear that repositioning authority and control within these relational networks can result in the democratisation of knowledge production, with the approach utilised by the present study providing opportunity for advancing a decolonised museum practice. Furthermore, that respect of and empathy for difference are central to an appropriate museology for today. Privilege was articulated through community and institutional priorities, opportunities and access to resources and this varied throughout the assemblage. Historically, mutually beneficial outcomes have resulted. Today epistemological and physical distance, resource limitations and external demands impact on responsiveness to opportunities that may be generated by the encounters between them. It must also be kept in mind that obligations to governance and the profession are contingent and political whereas cultural obligations transcend time and space. The final theme has revealed differences in value systems between museums and originating communities and the effect these differences have on their abilities to work towards a common purpose. This in turn contributes to our understanding of the assemblage components and the relational networks of which they are a part.

These findings show how the constituents of this assemblage are able to reform and reassemble into new social and material networks centred on knowledge, respect and opportunities, which I argue are central to an appropriate museology in the twenty-first century, a claim which will be addressed in the next chapter.

Notes

1 *Protected Objects Act 1975.*
2 Kaupapa Māori is a 'body of knowledge' distinctive to Māori people "accumulated by the experiences through history, of the Maori people" (Taki, 1996, p. 17). Kaupapa Māori methodology is participatory and acknowledges the legitimacy of Māori forms of knowledge (Smith, 1999, p. 205), with kaupapa Māori research considered that which is culturally safe, relevant and "undertaken by Māori, with Māori, for Māori" (ibid.) recognising that it can involve "the help of invited others" (Bishop, 2005, p. 113). It is in essence a philosophy that directs research methods to acknowledge and encompass Māori values, conceding that many intangible concepts, such as mana and mauri, "will only be partly understood and never completely known by non-Māori" (Pope, 2008, p. 70).

3 Te Papa leadership comprises the chief executive responsible for the conduct of the museum's operations and the kaihautū who leads the ongoing development of Te Papa's Māori tribal relationships, with bicultural policy based upon the partnership implicit in the Treaty of Waitangi between tangata whenua and tangata tiriti (Museum of New Zealand Te Papa Tongarewa, 2012/2013).
4 Pitt Rivers Museum. (1923). *Charles Smith Collection Related Documents File.* Oxford: Pitt Rivers Museum.
5 Translation of letter Tāmati Takarangi to Charles Smith, 26 December 1888, Whanganui Regional Museum collection 2017.34 Charles Smith Papers; MS 304.

References

Ames, M. M. (1999). How to decorate a house: The re-negotiation of cultural representations at the University of British Columbia Museum of Anthropology. *Museum Anthropology, 22*(3), 41–51.

Anonymous. (2013). Back to the future. *Upokopakaru.* Retrieved from http://upokopakaru.wordpress.com/2013/09/06/back-to-the-future/.

Atkinson, J. K. (2014). *Education, values and ethics in international heritage: Learning to respect.* Farnham: Ashgate Publishing Ltd.

Battiste, M. (2008). Research ethics for protecting indigenous knowledge and heritage: Institutional and researcher responsibilities. In N. K. Denzin, Y. S. Lincoln, & L. T. Smith (Eds.), *Handbook of critical and indigenous methodologies* (pp. 497–509). Los Angeles: Sage Publications.

Bishop, R. (2005). Freeing ourselves from neocolonial domination in research: A kaupapa Maori approach to creating knowledge. In N. K. Denzin & Y. S. Lincoln (Eds.), *The Sage handbook of qualitative research* (3rd ed., pp. 109–138). Thousand Oaks, CA: Sage Publications.

Bishop, R. (2008). Te Kotahitanga: Kaupapa Maori in mainstream classrooms. In N. K. Denzin, Y. S. Lincoln, & L. T. Smith (Eds.), *Handbook of critical and indigenous methodologies* (pp. 439–458). Los Angeles: Sage Publications.

Boast, R. (2011). Neocolonial collaboration: Museum as contact zone revisited. *Museum Anthropology, 34*(1), 56–70.

Butts, D., Dell, S., & Wills, R. (2002). Recent constitutional changes at the Whanganui Regional Museum. *Te Ara: Journal of Museums Aotearoa, 27*(2), 37–40.

Byrne, S. (2013). Exposing the "heart" of the museum: The archaeological sensibility in the storeroom. In R. Harrison, S. Byrne, & A. Clarke (Eds.), *Reassembling the collection: Indigenous agency and ethnographic collections* (pp. 199–228). New Mexico: School for Advanced Research (SAR) Press.

Clavir, M. (2002). *Preserving what is valued: Museums, conservation, and First Nations.* Vancouver: University of British Columbia Press.

Clifford, J. (1997). *Routes: Travel and translation in the late twentieth century.* Cambridge, MA: Harvard University Press.

Clifford, J. (2004). Looking several ways: Anthropology and native heritage in Alaska. *Current Anthropology, 45*(1), 5–30.

Clifford, J. (2010). *The times of the curator.* Paper presented at the The Task of the Curator: Translation, Intervention and Innovation in Exhibitionary Practice conference, University of California, Santa Cruz.

Erikson, P. P., Ward, H., & Wachendorf, K. (2002). *Voices of a thousand people: The Makah Cultural and Research Center*. Lincoln: University of Nebraska Press.

Golding, V., & Modest, W. (2013). *Museums and communities: Curators, collections and collaboration*. London: Bloomsbury.

Hakiwai, A. (2014). *He mana taonga, he mana tangata: Māori taonga and the politics of Māori tribal identity and development*. (PhD diss.), Victoria University of Wellington, Wellington. Retrieved from http://researcharchive.vuw.ac.nz/handle/10063/3709.

Harris, C., & O'Hanlon, M. (2013). The future of the enthnographic museum. *Anthropology Today, 29*(1), 8–12.

Harrison, R. (2013). Reassembling ethnographic museum collections. In R. Harrison, S. Byrne, & A. Clarke (Eds.), *Reassembling the collection: Indigenous agency and ethnographic collections* (pp. 3–35). New Mexico: School for Advanced Research (SAR) Press.

Hodder, I. (2003). The interpretation of documents and material culture. In N. K. Denzin & Y. S. Lincoln (Eds.), *Collecting and interpreting qualitative materials* (2nd ed., pp. 155–175). Thousand Oaks, CA: Sage Publications.

Horwood, M. (2017). Going digital in the GLAM sector: ICT innovations & collaborations for taonga Māori. In H. Whaanga, M. Apperley, & T. T. Keegan (Eds.), *Te whare hangarau Māori: Language, culture and technology* (pp. 149–164). Hamilton: University of Waikato.

Kramer, J. (2006). *Switchbacks: Art, ownership, and Nuxalk national identity*. Vancouver: University of British ColumbiaPress.

Kreps, C. F. (2003). *Liberating culture: Cross-cultural perspectives on museums, curation and heritage preservation*. London: Routledge.

Kreps, C. F. (2011). Changing the rules of the road: Post-colonialism and the new ethics of museum anthropology. In J. Marstine (Ed.), *Routledge companion to museum ethics: Redefining ethics for the twenty-first century museum* (pp. 70–84). London: Routledge.

Krmpotich, C., Peers, L. L., Haida Repatriation Committee, & staff of the Pitt Rivers Museum and British Museum. (2013). *This is our life: Haida material heritage and changing museum practice*. Vancouver: University of British Columbia Press.

Lonetree, A. (2012). *Decolonizing museums: Representing Native America in national and tribal museums*. Chapel Hill, NC: University of North Carolina Press.

Loza, C. B., & Quispe, W. Á. (2009). Report on the Niño Korin Collection at the Museum of World Culture. Describing, naming and classifying medical objects from the Tiwanaku Period. In A. Muñoz (Ed.), *The power of labelling. Report to Kulturrådet, Arts Council Norway* (pp. 59–75).

Lynch, B. T. (2011a). Collaboration, contestation, and creative conflict: On the efficacy of museum/community partnerships. In J. Marstine (Ed.), *Routledge companion to museum ethics: Redefining ethics for the twenty-first century museum* (pp. 146–163). London: Routledge.

Lynch, B. T. (2011b). Custom-made reflective practice: Can museums realise their capabilities in helping others realise theirs? *Museum Management and Curatorship, 26*(5), 441–458.

Lynch, B. T. (2013). Reflective debate, radical transparency and trust in the museum. *Museum Management and Curatorship*, 28(1), 1–13.

Lynch, B. T. (2014). "Generally dissatisfied": Hidden pedagogy in the postcolonial museum. *THEMA. La revue des Musées de la civilisation*, 1, 79–92.

Lynch, B. T., & Alberti, S. J. M. M. (2010). Legacies of prejudice: Racism, co-production and radical trust in the museum. *Museum Management and Curatorship*, 25(1), 13–35.

Macdonald, S. (2002). On "old things"" The fetishization of past everyday life. In N. Rapport (Ed.), *An anthropology of Britain* (pp. 89–106). Oxford: Berg.

Manatū Taonga Ministry for Culture and Heritage. (2017). *Manatū Taonga Ministry for Culture and Heritage Annual Report 2016–17: Pūrongo ā-Tau*. Wellington: Manatū Taonga Ministry for Culture and Heritage.

Marstine, J. (Ed.). (2011). *Routledge companion to museum ethics: Redefining ethics for the twenty-first century museum*. London: Routledge.

McCall, V., & Gray, C. (2013). Museums and the "new museology": Theory, practice and organisational change. *Museum Management and Curatorship*, 29(1), 19–35.

McKenzie, M. (1993). A challenge to museums – keeping the taonga warm. *Zeitschrift fur Ethnologie*, 118, 79–85.

Mead, S. M. (2003). *Tikanga Maori: Living by Maori values*. Wellington: Huia.

Merriman, N. (2000). *Beyond the glass case: The past, the heritage, and the public*. London: Institute of Archaeology, University College.

Mignolo, W. D. (2009). Preface to the report on Niño Korin collection. In A. Muñoz (Ed.), *The power of labelling: Report to Kulturrådet, Arts Council Norway*. Norway: Kulturrådet.

Mignolo, W. D. (2011). *The darker side of western modernity: Global futures, decolonial options*. Durham, NC: Duke University Press.

Mignolo, W. D. (2013). Enacting the archives, decentering the museums: The Museum of Islamic Art in Doha and the Asian Civilizations Museum in Singapore. *Contemporary Visual Culture in North Africa and the Middle East*, 006. Retrieved from www.ibraaz.org/essays/77.

Muñoz, A. (2009). *The power of labelling: Report to Kulturrådet, Arts Council Norway*. Norway: Kulturrådet.

Museum of New Zealand Te Papa Tongarewa. (2012/2013). *Te Pūrongo ā Tau Annual Report*. Wellington: Museum of New Zealand.

Museum of New Zealand Te Papa Tongarewa. (2015). *Māori collection*. Retrieved from www.tepapa.govt.nz/ResearchAtTePapa/CollectionCareAndAccess/History OfCollections/Pages/Maoricollection.aspx.

Office of Treaty Settlements. (2014). *Ruruku whakatupua: The Whanganui Iwi deed of settlement in relation to the Whanganui River*. Wellington: Ministry of Justice.

Onciul, B. (2011). *Unsettling assumptions about community engagement: A new perspective on indigenous Blackfoot participation in museums and heritage sites in Alberta, Canada*. (PhD diss.), Newcastle University, Newcastle. Retrieved from http://hdl.handle.net/10443/1401.

Onciul, B. (2015). *Museums, heritage and indigenous voice: Decolonizing engagement*. New York: Routledge.

Peers, L. L., & Brown, A. K. (Eds.). (2003). *Museums and source communities: A Routledge reader*. London: Routledge.

Pope, C. C. (2008). Kaupapa Māori research, supervision and uncertainty: "What's a Pākehā fella to do?" In P. Liamputtong (Ed.), *Doing cross-cultural research: Ethical and methodological perspectives* (pp. 71–81). Dordrecht: Springer.

Prown, J. D. (1982). Mind in matter: An introduction to material culture theory and method. *Winterthur Portfolio, 17*(1), 1–19.

Qureshi, S. (2011). *Peoples on parade: Exhibitions, empire and anthropology in nineteenth century Britain*. Chicago: University of Chicago Press.

Salmond, A. (1984). Nga huarahi o te ao Maori: Pathways in the Maori world. In S. M. Mead (Ed.), *Te Maori: Maori art from New Zealand collections* (pp. 109–137). Auckland: Heinemann.

Salmond, A. (2017). *Tears of Rangi: Experiments across worlds*. Auckland: Auckland University Press.

Sandahl, J., & Mignolo, W. D. (2013 May, 22). *The future of ethnographic museums: A public conversation*. Gothenburg: Critical Curatorship Workshop, University of Gothenburg.

Schorch, P., & Hakiwai, A. (2014). Mana taonga and the public sphere: A dialogue between indigenous practice and western theory. *International Journal of Cultural Studies, 17*(2), 191–205.

Sharpe, L., & Wilson, C. (Writers). (2007). *Te Pihi Mata – The Sacred Eye* exhibition [Exhibition text]. Whanganui: Whanganui Regional Museum.

Smith, L. T. (1999). *Decolonizing methodologies: Research and indigenous peoples*. London: Zed Books.

Sully, D. (2007). *Decolonising conservation: Caring for Maori meeting houses outside New Zealand*. Walnut Creek, CA: Left Coast Press.

Taki, M. (1996). *Kaupapa Māori and contemporary iwi resistance*. (MA Thesis), University of Auckland, Auckland.

Tapsell, P. (1997). The flight of Pareraututu. *Journal of the Polynesian Society, 104*(4), 223–374.

Tapsell, P. (2006). *Ko tawa: Maori treasures of New Zealand*. Auckland: David Bateman.

Tapsell, P. (2011). "Aroha mai: Whose museum?" The rise of indigenous ethics within museum contexts: A Maori-tribal perspective. In J. Marstine (Ed.), *Routledge companion to museum ethics: Redefining ethics for the twenty-first century museum* (pp. 85–111). London: Routledge.

4 Working together

There's been a fire ignited within the hearts of those that went . . . They've started something. It's now time to keep that connected.

Che Wilson[1]

Through this research I have sought to find solutions to the difficulties some Māori tribal communities in New Zealand face accessing their ancestral heritage housed in museums when it is located offshore. I proposed that increased awareness of the different cultural perspectives and knowledge systems of a Māori tribal community in New Zealand and a museum community in England over time would improve understanding of the value and meaning of Māori heritage items to both groups today. This in turn, I argued, would contribute to identifying ways and means for these communities to negotiate ongoing relationships when they are remotely located and unable to engage in face-to-face interactions. I have also argued that this study is important because, even though a decolonised museology has been evident for several decades in a variety of ways, there is little *ongoing* engagement between indigenous communities and collecting institutions where geographic distance isolates these groups from one another.

I employed a kaupapa Māori approach to enable a Pākehā, in a study centred on a collection of Māori heritage items with a Māori community as a primary research stakeholder, to acknowledge and incorporate Māori values into the research strategy. I also positioned and grounded this research in current museum practice, contextualised within the New Zealand situation through my experience working with communities as a museum professional. By exploring and documenting a detailed, situated case study I was able to determine the impact of diverse value systems and epistemologies (indigenous, academic, museum – New Zealand and England) on the access to heritage objects over time and through space. The overall value of this research is in the grounding of the lessons from the Relational Museum and assemblage theory analyses (which have mostly been directed at historical collecting), in contemporary museum-community engagement by showing that the actor-networks are ongoing and that indigenous assemblages continue to form and reform as a result of interactions between their component parts. This reassembling is visible in contemporary indigenous re-engagement with their museum-held heritage, and will be ongoing in potential future interactions between any and all of the assemblage components.

Utilising a theoretical framework adopted by Harrison and others in the volume *Reassembling the Collection*, I was particularly interested in examining a number of entities that fell out of the disassembly of the research network at the centre of this study. Identifying, analysing and discussing these entities, which are temporally and spatially contingent, and manifest in terms of power and values, helped to answer the research problem posed.

This study has shown that new meanings can arise from the analysis of an assemblage that incorporates temporal and spatial factors, in this case when material culture is separated from its original context. By expanding this model through the re-engagement of indigenous human and non-human actors, I have demonstrated that the collapsing of distance in space-time is possible and thus the reinserting of object-actors, or taonga, into indigenous narratives.

What can we learn from this?

The findings from this study therefore make several contributions to the current literature. First, documentation of the dynamic interactions of these disassembled entities through time and space resulted in a shift in thinking about the way power was distributed within and among these assemblages. In this way it was possible to bridge epistemological and physical distances between a Māori tribal community and an English museum, which can be applied to indigenous communities and museums more broadly. The decolonisation of museum practice I propose can be advanced through a disassembly-reassembly theoretical framework. A significant contribution of this research is therefore the development of an indigenous engagement praxis for museums with ethnographic collections located remotely from originating communities (see Table 4.1).

Second, from this study it is clear that the repositioning of authority and control within these relational networks can result in the democratisation of knowledge production, with respect and empathy for difference, as shown in Chapter 3, clearly central to a decolonised museology. Also, bringing together the range of skill sets that have emerged from this assemblage illustrates the creative and generative potential of a heritage network. Privilege, in terms of priorities, opportunities and resources,

Table 4.1 Praxis for indigenous engagement with remotely located ethnographic museum collections.

Identify shared objectives at outset to promote co-operative and democratic knowledge production

Integrate culture-specific classification systems

Increase movement of knowledge/improve access to museum-held knowledge

Support measures to equalise power relations – shared resources, repositioned authority

Give recognition to knowledge framed in multiple ways

Refer to expertise of other epistemologies; bring together different skill sets

Approach museum practice (political and operational) as a shared responsibility

---

varies throughout this assemblage. This was evident historically, when mutually beneficial outcomes resulted from bringing together network components. Today, epistemological and physical distance between the components, as well as resource limitations and external demands, impact on responsiveness to any opportunities the encounters between them may generate.

Third, the changing role of significant and utilitarian taonga over time is also clearly illustrated, with the most significant purpose of historical actions being the strengthening of relationships. Today, the contemporary agents within these indigenous assemblages reposition themselves to re-engage with their object-ancestors and their current custodians. To focus upon the perception that for Māori people 'things,' even in their absence, are active community members is one way to move beyond the politics of indigenous representation (as did Harrison et al., 2013), with a range of mechanism used in the past to alter the trajectory of certain objects for the future benefit of the community.

Furthermore, the study reinforces the idea that taonga *objectify* social relationships, a characteristic of Māori gift-giving, and enact relationships prompting contemporary responses from human actors. Thus the contemporary interactions of the human and non-human indigenous actors, which take place within the social and material networks that are museums, represent the *continuity* of relationships objectified by their ancestors. At the same time recognising the temporary nature of these human actors in the trajectory of these object-ancestors over time.

Fourth, while museums may respect notions of animacy and material agency, taonga are unequivocally regarded by Māori as tapu, animate and capable of effecting relationships. As such, taonga have a mauri, an energy that binds and animates. Mauri is present in all things in the physical world and is a force which interconnects all things in some way with one another. As the Waitangi Tribunal Whanganui River Report (1999, p. 39) states

> all things have a mauri, a life-force and personality of their own, and it was certainly the case that a river was seen to be so endowed . . . [This] was to be respected [or] . . . it would lose its vitality and force, and its kindred people, those who depend on it would ultimately suffer. Again, it was to be respected as though it were one's close kin.

One outcome of the Whanganui River Report for Whanganui River iwi, was the recognition given to the Whanganui River of legal personhood, officially passing into law in 2017 (Te Awa Tupua (Whanganui River Claims Settlement) Bill). Barlow (1991, p. 83) describes the importance of the maintenance of the mauri for the wellbeing of a river and the environment as a whole providing as an example how the depletion of the food supply in a river, can decrease the mauri or health of that food supply. This sits with Malafouris' (2013) argument for a symmetrical collaboration between humans and things where agency is the relational and emergent product of our engagement with the world rather than solely an attribute of humanity.

However, while Malafouris is explaining the interdependence of human and material agency, the value of this approach for the present study is the equal weighting given to material culture in social relations, which is an essential quality of the principle of mauri within a Māori world view. By entwining the physical and spiritual qualities of a thing, mauri provides a parallel praxis with this Western theoretical framework for explaining equality and symmetry between the components of a relational network. It thus provides the author, as a Pākehā scholar-curator, with a means by which to integrate such intangibles respectfully. Because these, as Pope (2008, p. 70) states, "will only be partly understood and never completely known by non-Māori" and cannot be easily uplifted and inserted into another world view. This theoretical innovation, a synthesis of Māori and Western thought, also enables understanding of how relationships between network constituents can be objectified with the transformation of objects from passive things to active actor-entities inspiring contemporary responses from descendant communities, their human-actor kin.

As discussed in Chapter 3, the recognition that connectedness with taonga goes deeper than a physical reconnection with a thing, and the response to issues of access to and use of taonga in New Zealand by Māori communities can be seen in innovative solutions such as the Mana Taonga principle at Te Papa, constitutional reform at the Whanganui Regional Museum and the adoption of He Korahi Māori (a Māori dimension) and Teu le Vā (a Pacific dimension) by the Auckland Museum trust board. Also, various regional approaches to an emerging indigenous museology are practised in museums which recognise kaitiakitanga or guardianship over indigenous collections. Similar strategies have been instituted in other post-settler nation-states. Although museums in Britain and elsewhere in Europe are expanding experiences for indigenous engagement, the continuity of strategies relies upon individual and institutional commitment, which may be transitory. Moreover, conventional ownership of items in museum collections is generally legal and binding.

Fifth, Chapter 3 identified and presented a number of current challenges in museum practice when geographic distance is a factor, both for museum professionals in England and for Māori originating communities in New Zealand. I have shown that immediacy in time and closeness across space sustains indigene–museum relationships through face-to-face interactions and empowering communities, and that this was supported by institutional practices and policies. In contrast, distance constrains the development and maintenance of these relationships, with the result that interactions were intermittent, anonymous and formal, and museum-led projects were prioritised. In New Zealand, it is clear that the proximity of Māori communities and museums and the impact of Māori autonomy on museum practice over the past three decades have led to opportunities for effective collaborative practice. In England, on the other hand, museum responsiveness does not prioritise indigenous communities from elsewhere over its immediate and often diverse communities and institutional stakeholders, and professional priorities may naturally rest elsewhere.

Chapter 3 also discussed differences in value systems between entity components and the effects these have on the relational network. I concluded that a mutually beneficial relationship can develop between entities, but only if each is prepared to work towards a common purpose. For this to be effective, originating communities must employ strategies that continue to instil their cultural values in the museum at distance, by proactively maintaining relationships with the institutional custodians of their patrimony, and guiding them in the care of this heritage to ensure the cultural safety of both the object-ancestors and the people they come into contact with. Importantly, institutional staff, as transitory guardians, also have a moral responsibility to safeguard this cultural patrimony in ethically responsive and culturally respectful ways. Likewise, as the singular access point to this material for communities of origin or other institutional publics, they have a responsibility to facilitate this access in appropriate ways. Working towards a common purpose, I suggest, is possible once differences in value systems are acknowledged. However, while projects can be catalysts for relationships, their longevity relies upon other factors, and museums and communities must therefore develop mechanisms for continuity of post-project interactions to counter one-off projects and perpetuate relationships.

A new approach

This new theoretical and practice-based approach involving an in-depth, situated case study analysed over time, comparing and contrasting cultural perspectives, provides new insights into relationships between originating communities and remotely located museums holding collections of their heritage. These findings add to our understanding of *appropriate museology*; defined by Kreps (2008, p. 23) as "an approach to museum development and training that adapts museum practices and strategies for cultural heritage preservation to local cultural contexts and socioeconomic conditions." I propose situating this *appropriate museology* within the relational network made up of an ethnographic museum and an indigenous community by reframing it to reflect the network components more aptly. Thus an appropriate museology in this context embraces an indigenous one, where indigenous and museological (Western) knowledge systems and cultural practices are given equal ranking and can operate in parallel within an organisation.

As suggested in the previous chapter, differences in value systems were reformed into new networks centred upon knowledge, respect and opportunities. On the basis of this evidence, I put forward the idea of a praxis for indigenous engagement with museums (see Table 4.1). Thus acknowledging these different value systems, I identified the benefits of each for a collection of heritage items. These findings suggest opportunities for future research, which museum and indigenous stakeholders can continue to explore; that is, whether a focussed and detailed study of the relationships these heritage items generate can result in more than a one-off project for a museum and a community.

This study contributes to "new conceptions of relationships of care and curation" promoted by Kreps (2003), Byrne and others (2011). The value of these new approaches is the movement of heritage items from decontextualisation to a recontextualisation in which a transformation takes place within museological practice; from a salvage and rescue paradigm to a more "inclusive, collaborative, and culturally relative" one (Kreps, 2006, p. 458). Harrison (2013, p. 5) has considered the metaphorical (affective, political, historical) as well as the physical weight of objects in museum collections as a more "sophisticated approach to agency and the fields of material and social relations that constitute the contemporary museum and its histories" so as to arrive at new notions of museum object care and curation. However, the present study has taken a step further, through the incorporation of a nuanced analysis of the differences between value systems, to approach museum curation as a shared responsibility between originating communities and museum staff.

Furthermore, my work contributes to the literatures on museums and originating communities by documenting the dynamic interactions between these communities, over time and through space, up until the present. This new approach provides the opportunity for a better understanding of the differences between these communities, and of the ways in which innovative solutions to engagement and empowerment have been adopted by institutions to address this. It also advances a decolonised museum position based on the democratisation of knowledge production in the indigene–museum network, where our difficult histories are acknowledged and communicated, and the epistemological distance is effectively reduced so as to promote partnership opportunities. Moreover, the mediatory effects of recent reconnection with taonga and their affective impact have facilitated contemporary relationship-building and contributed to advancement of tribal identity.

Tapsell (2011, pp. 86–87) questions whether the value of objects in museums in terms of ancestral relationships to communities of origin has been fully explored in museological discourse. I propose that findings from the research, combined with my own professional experience, in conjunction with advancements in museum studies, furthers understanding of the meaning of objects to specific communities within this discourse. As a result, it is possible to forge new ways for indigenous communities to enhance and perpetuate relationships with museums holding collections of their ancestral heritage.

From these findings I conclude the following are factors that have implications for museum practice,

first, relationship-building is generally project-led and museum initiated,
second, indigenous people rarely prioritise academic achievement in this field,
third, indigenous people rarely hold positions of power in museums, and,
fourth the scale of museum collections inhibits proactive relationship-building with individual communities.

In the contemporary context, preferred outcomes differ between network constituents and only time will now tell whether perpetuity of relationships is in fact embedded in the objects, as suggested by Coote. It is clear that taonga in museum collections are reliant on projects to maintain their active nature. Furthermore, while distance precludes regular interaction, outcomes are more likely to result from face-to-face encounters between indigenous and museum-community members than any other sort of engagement. However, relationships between these groups are unlikely to persist when there is significant geographic distance unless an individual from the museum or originating community is prepared to maintain that relationships through regular and ongoing communication and successfully prioritises resources for its maintenance, or they can formalise an agreement institutionalising the relationship. Moreover, respectful relationships develop from mutual trust. Results suggest true reciprocity (through manaakitanga/care, support, hospitality and democratic knowledge production) is an essential element, and time an important factor.

Finally, there are many pressing issues for museums and indigenous communities that compete for resources, with the focus of each towards different priorities. While Ngā Paerangi's collective history, as for many indigenous groups, has been one of depopulation, dislocation and dispersal, with the disruption of traditional tribal-based networks a consequence of historical experiences (colonisation, impact on health, land loss, assimilationist policies, loss of economic base, ongoing economic marginality, cultural loss, language loss, population decline), they are facing new challenges and opportunities effected by processes such as the Waitangi Tribunal. For the Pitt Rivers Museum, as for most museums, resources are limited and the institution struggles with being constantly confronted with new and often competing opportunities.

Therefore, a specific insight from this research is that even though each indigenous community and each museum is unique, there are some common approaches, which scholars and professionals anywhere can learn. These common issues will enable constituents to reform and reassemble into new social and material networks centred on respect and new knowledge, which have the potential to generate opportunities for the future.

Respect: During this study I set out to determine the meaning of heritage items over time to entities within a relational network and whether this could impact on the nature of contemporary relationships between human actors. The results of this study indicate that respect is a fundamental principle of such embryonic relationships, as Ponga (personal communication, 18 August 2013) stated, "this is nothing to do with our cultural values, this is everything to do with the relationship-building between two human beings and respect is everything." Clifford (2004, p. 6) also asserts that,

> even the most severe indigenous critics of anthropology recognize the potential for alliances when they are based on shared resources, repositioned indigenous and academic authorities, and relations of genuine respect.

Genuine respect entails a willingness to take into account the relationship partner's point of view, their world view, and their values (Patterson, 1992, p. 10) and for this to occur requires willingness, enthusiasm and potentially also learning and applying cultural protocols. This study's findings suggest, however, that respect was not enough to cement these relationships in the long-term. Nevertheless, I also discovered that taonga embody social relationships and generate new ones. These social relationships can be manifest in the historical transactions that resulted in their movement through a gift or exchange network into a museum collection, or more recently in the re-engagement of descendant communities. Most importantly, they will be ongoing in potential future interactions between any and all of these relational entities when all the fundamental requirements for a relationship come together; as Clifford stated previously – resources, repositioned authority and genuine respect.

New knowledge: Importantly, this study generated new knowledge for the human actors as well as to the field of museum studies and the discipline of anthropology. The research provides qualitative data about differences between Western and Māori epistemologies around the value of taonga and recognises that place-based approaches have their own distinctive and embedded value systems. There is also a range of contributions to knowledge specific to individual objects and people and their interconnectivity including expanded biographies – human and object – and cultural capital, culture-specific practices for museum staff and tribal members, and the centrality of face-to-face encounters with taonga for the revitalisation of cultural heritage practices.

Opportunities for the future: It is clear that the loss of cultural heritage impacts upon identity. Taonga, as symbols of Māori identity, therefore can "reunite and empower the most important resources of all: people" which museums as custodians of heritage are well positioned to assist with (Tapsell, 2003, p. 250). Hakiwai (2014, p. ii) reiterates this point in his doctoral thesis when he concluded that taonga play a pivotal role "in informing and shaping tribal development futures." This research identified a number of potential opportunities for ongoing, emerging assemblages. Reflecting on past events and their consequences enhances understanding of actions of ancestors, strengthening current decision-making; furthering the embryonic relationships established in 2013 individually and collectively; expanding museum communication strategies to include indigenous contextualization; and identifying opportunities for reciprocation of manaakitanga (hospitality), reinsertion of taonga into cultural practices, digital repatriation, and disseminating outcomes from shared experiences for others to learn from.

Significantly, although ethnographic material in museums is often considered a reminder of colonisation and cultural loss, reengaging with the Charles

Smith collection for Ngā Paerangi was considered a positive experience, as the collection represents a physical embodiment of their past that has survived to empower *new* histories and relationships today and into the future.

The ideas discussed in this chapter are brought together in Table 4.1 as potential praxis for community members, academic and museological practitioners when forging relationships based around indigenous cultural heritage collections.

In this chapter I have looked at the implications of the results of this study in relation to museum–indigenous community relationships. Further research might well be conducted in order to explore the way in which indigenous communities can work towards developing relationships with museums in perpetuity when distance is a factor. However, we must keep in mind that "any account of assemblage is, of course, inevitably partial – it is never possible to follow all of the chains of connections that might be involved" (Macdonald, 2011, p. 127). While the potential for many strands of the current analysis to have continued on many different trajectories is inevitable, I have endeavoured to restrict the elements of this study to those with a pragmatic application for the research stakeholders, who may themselves encounter opportunities to explore these tantalising trajectories at some point in the future.

Museums are doing important work unpacking their documentation history so they can disseminate information about what they have. In some cases they are also proactively seeking out original owner communities to establish contemporary relationships. Importantly, studying ethnographic items or collections that are linked to specific named communities and communicating this information can have a profound impact on community identity. More studies that explore mechanisms through which this can be achieved are important.

The disassembly-reassembly theoretical framework applied to this research has resulted in a significant academic contribution to museum studies. It has revealed the emergence of an indigenous engagement praxis resulting from the first contextualised study of a heritage assemblage over time, which shows that actor-networks are ongoing and that indigenous assemblages continue to form and reform as a result of interactions between their component parts. This praxis, combining a range of developments in contemporary museum practice for museum–indigenous community engagement which have proved effective in New Zealand and other settler-colonies, has application elsewhere for relationship-building between indigenous communities and the custodians of their museum-held heritage when distance is a factor.

In the final concluding chapter I return to the questions about museum practice and the implications for museum–indigenous community relationships with which the book began. I consider where to from here for the future of indigenous authority for museum-held collections.

Note

1 Personal communication, 12 December 2013.

References

Barlow, C. (1991). *Tikanga whakaaro: Key concepts in Maori culture*. Auckland: Oxford University Press.

Byrne, S., Clarke, A., Harrison, R., & Torrence, R. (Eds.). (2011). *Unpacking the collection: Networks of material and social agency in the museum*. New York: Springer.

Clifford, J. (2004). Looking several ways: Anthropology and native heritage in Alaska. *Current Anthropology, 45*(1), 5–30.

Hakiwai, A. (2014). *He mana taonga, he mana tangata: Māori taonga and the politics of Māori tribal identity and development*. (PhD diss.), Victoria University of Wellington, Wellington. Retrieved from http://researcharchive.vuw.ac.nz/handle/10063/3709.

Harrison, R. (2013). Reassembling ethnographic museum collections. In R. Harrison, S. Byrne, & A. Clarke (Eds.), *Reassembling the collection: Indigenous agency and ethnographic collections* (pp. 3–35). New Mexico: School for Advanced Research (SAR) Press.

Kreps, C. F. (2003). *Liberating culture: Cross-cultural perspectives on museums, curation and heritage preservation*. London: Routledge.

Kreps, C. F. (2006). Non-western models of museums and curation in cross-cultural perspective. In S. Macdonald (Ed.), *A companion to museum studies* (pp. 457–472). Oxford: Wiley-Blackwell.

Kreps, C. F. (2008). Appropriate museology in theory and practice. *Museum Management and Curatorship, 23*(1), 23–41.

Macdonald, S. (2011). Reassembling Nuremberg, reassembling heritage. In T. Bennett & C. Healy (Eds.), *Assembling culture* (pp. 113–130). London: Routledge.

Malafouris, L. (2013). *How things shape the mind: A theory of material engagement*. Cambridge, MA: MIT Press.

Patterson, J. (1992). *Exploring Maori values*. Palmerston North: Dunmore Press.

Pope, C. C. (2008). Kaupapa Māori research, supervision and uncertainty: "What's a Pākehā fella to do?" In P. Liamputtong (Ed.), *Doing cross-cultural research ethical and methodological perspectives* (pp. 71–81). Dordrecht: Springer.

Tapsell, P. (2003). Afterword: Beyond the frame. In L. L. Peers & A. K. Brown (Eds.), *Museums and source communities: A Routledge reader* (pp. 242–251). London: Routledge.

Tapsell, P. (2011). "Aroha mai: Whose museum?" The rise of indigenous ethics within museum contexts: A Maori-tribal perspective. In J. Marstine (Ed.), *Routledge companion to museum ethics: Redefining ethics for the twenty-first century museum* (pp. 85–111). London: Routledge.

Waitangi Tribunal. (1999). *The Whanganui River Report WAI167*. Wellington: GB Publications.

Conclusion

In this book I have shown that the concept of shared, negotiated ownership has evolved further in New Zealand museums than in museums in England, specifically with regard to taonga. This evolution is reflected through museum acknowledgement and understanding of tribal kaitiakitanga (guardianship). In this way New Zealand museum professionals are more naturally comfortable than their British colleagues with the claims to ownership that Māori individuals and communities make, whether legal or cultural, and have developed a range of mechanisms to support aspirations for self-determination over heritage management, including repatriation policies. Acknowledgement of kaitiakitanga is also manifest through the employment of indigenous staff as discussed elsewhere (for example, Butts, 2007; Hakiwai, 1999; McCarthy, 2011). This complex and contested area is, however, not as easily accommodated by our colleagues from museums in England, who of course do not work in proximity to originating communities but are instead exposed to those who proactively seek out their heritage held offshore.

A praxis for indigenous engagement

While this book describes a context-specific case study, the lessons learned here have broader application. I contend that for the contemporary museum to apply any one of the elements of the praxis proposed in the preceding chapter, this will contribute to the development and maintenance of frameworks of meaningful engagement with indigenous originating communities. Out of this, new forms of collaborative partnerships may be developed between holding institutions and remotely located originating communities for indigenous cultural heritage collections.

In the volume of essays focussed upon museum-indigenous community interactions, Silverman (2015, p. 10) highlights the importance of identifying aspirations of all stakeholders at the outset for success in collaborative projects. I propose taking this further. By identifying *shared objectives* at the outset of a project, the first element of this praxis will promote co-operative and democratic knowledge production and positive outcomes for project partners. Allowing the time and creating the space to negotiate these objectives are essential factors. It takes time to build a relationship and gain respect and trust from individuals and communities and outcomes may not be realised for years. As Bienkowski (2015, p. 441) has noted, stakeholders need the time to be able to weigh the benefits of participating (or not) and fully understand the processes and expectations involved without feeling that they are fitting into a schedule with outcomes pre-determined by other parties. Decades of prior relationships and joint projects enabled a partnership between Ngā Paerangi and the author to exist and for this project to be undertaken.

There are numerous examples of projects exploring the integration of culture-specific classification systems, the second element of this praxis, which have resulted in a range of outcomes for indigenous stakeholders and museums, such as engaging "indigenous discourse about historical heritage" by tracing the changing indigenous terminology for objects (Bohaker, Ojiig Corbiere, & Phillips, 2015, p. 56), or by providing culturally appropriate sharing and access protocols for cultural knowledge management using content management systems such as Mukurtu (Christen, 2015). Placing objects within an indigenous cultural framework through their renaming can contribute to the reclamation of cultural ownership (McCarthy, 2011, p. 126), and in this way time, place, people and action are combined to enhance meaning and reveal relationships. This is further illustrated at Auckland Museum where processes developed to achieve two major collection access projects, Te Awe and the Pacific Collection Access Project, have established standards of practice that are applicable for any collecting institution housing ethnographic material. In the words of Matai Edmonds (2018), curator working in the Te Awe team,

> the ethnographic framework that has historically been used to organise the taonga Māori collections is now being recast. Instead a Mātauranga Māori approach is being developed by our collections team that recovers taonga names and redefines the relationships they have with each other.

Supporting stakeholder communities to navigate the social and material networks of the museum will increase movement of knowledge and improve access to museum-held knowledge, the third element of this praxis. Online databases have contributed to the increasing awareness by many indigenous communities of their material heritage held in museum collections both locally and globally. Similarly the development of digital platforms and databases has facilitated the return of cultural information and objects to many communities (Horwood, 2017). Likewise encouraging knowledge generation by and for consumption of originating communities, which is currently most notable where indigenous advocacy intersects with museum practice, rather than prioritising Western scholars and audiences, will further improve access to museum-held knowledge.

A range of measures can be supported to equalise power relations in the museum, illustrating the fourth element of this praxis. Employing indigenous curators, individuals who possess double knowledge systems and can navigate within and between museums and communities, is a priority in many New Zealand museums. Others have found using Web 2.0 social networking technologies as a forum, a successful strategy for progressing relationship-building by 'disprivileging' the museum as the exclusive site of authority (Basu, 2015, p. 348).

Additionally, while unwrapping the legacies of the colonial project may be uncomfortable, thinking about the circumstances in which objects moved from community to museum collection, taking into account potential for indigenous agency in these historical transactions, can add to our understanding of these often conflicted and not fully explored spaces and relationships. Assigning primacy to the processes of collection formation can be beneficial in drawing attention to the ways in which the historical network constituents interacted.

I have demonstrated that recognising knowledge framed in multiple ways, identified as the fifth element of this praxis, can be achieved by acknowledging that authenticity and meaning are negotiable and constructed and that "the enrichment of knowledge is not achieved through the contest of one knowledge with another" (Basu, 2015, p. 348). While recognition of this can lead to the development of mutually beneficial relationships, I caution that this will only occur if each is prepared to work towards a common purpose. The co-creation of a digital heritage network structured around different knowledge systems that emerged out of a Cambridge Museum of Archaeology & Anthropology–Toi Hauiti partnership (Lythberg, Hogsden, & Ngata, 2017) exemplifies this. This network resulted in enhanced museum-held knowledge while also bringing collections into indigenous-controlled digital space.

Using a number of studies and my own experience as a museum professional, I have demonstrated a range of strategies for successfully applying the sixth element of this praxis, bringing expertise of other knowledge and value systems as well as different skill sets together, for the benefit of meaningful engagement between indigenous communities and museums. By opening our minds to other ways of seeing the world and the place of human and non-human actors within it, opportunities can be made for recovering knowledge embedded in objects to restore and revitalise traditional practices, knowledge can be made accessible more broadly especially to those who would benefit most directly from it, and cultural safety for the taonga and those who encounter them can be enhanced. Additionally, combining curatorial and indigenous approaches to classification of objects can facilitate reorganising of object records to be meaningful within indigenous knowledge systems.

Many factors can positively contribute to the ways and means in which museum practice is approached as a shared responsibility, the final element of the praxis proposed in the preceding chapter. These include among other things, shifting control of representation and use of meaning, acknowledging community and institutional perspectives, moving from co-operative, consultative or collaborative practices to partnerships, and instituting mechanisms – procedures, policies – for applying principles of democratised museum practice. The Whanganui Regional Museum's policy, for example, relating to collection access and use devolves responsibility for decision-making, when appropriate, to designated individuals or groups established through formalised relationship agreements with cultural owners. Auckland Museum has instituted similar processes for use of Māori images from the collection (O'Donovan & Richardson, 2017). Return of important cultural treasures on long-term loan to Hawai'i by Te Papa in 2017 resulting in significant outcomes including "new processes of cultural recovery and self-determination for contemporary Hawaiians" (Mallon et al., 2017, p. 5) certainly validates institutional commitment to creatively and constructively approaching these incredibly difficult and complex issues.

In this book I have proposed a method for indigenous engagement with museum collections, combining a range of developments in contemporary museum practice for community engagement, to address the legacy of historic ethnographic collecting for indigenous communities and museums. I have also suggested ways that may guide community members, academics and museological practitioners when forging relationships based around indigenous cultural heritage. I contend that by negotiating power and authority within a relational network of indigenous community and museum, alongside acknowledging and communicating our difficult histories, together we can move from collaborative approaches to shared authority and indigenous self-determination in the museum sphere, and progress the task of decolonising the museum in practice.

I hope that other indigenous originating communities and museums can learn from the experiences of Ngā Paerangi people documented here and take these lessons further within their own spheres of experience and engagement.

Epilogue

In August 2016 I received an email from Clare Fazan, a distant relative of Charles Smith, who had come across several packets of letters in a suitcase given to her by an aunt several years previously. The material was to and from Charles Smith to family back in England and from his Māori neighbours at Kaiwhāiki. Clare, while searching online sources for information about this distant relative, came across my contact details.

Discussions with the Pitt Rivers and Whanganui Regional Museum staff about the most suitable outcome for this material followed. One year later these packets of letters, notes and maps were received back in Whanganui by members of Ngā Paerangi iwi as a gift to the museum from Clare Fazan. They provide a wealth of new information about the taonga Smith collected, his experiences in New Zealand, his relationships at Kaiwhāiki on the Whanganui River and also significantly a voice for some of the indigenous actors in the relational network described in this book. The museum staff are working with Ngā Paerangi members around kaitiakitanga arrangements for this new material. In January 2018 Clare and her husband Richard Rawlings visited New Zealand and were welcomed at Kaiwhāiki Marae where they met the descendants of Te Oti Takarangi, Wiremu Pātene and other Ngā Paerangi people, and visited the site of Charles Smith's homestead at Te Korito.

This significant and surprising outcome again reminds me that for Māori these gifts symbolise an enduring relationship that can span generations. The recent reforming of this relational assemblage at Kaiwhāiki further exemplifies the Māori values embedded in the original gifts to Charles Smith, with the knowledge recovered within these letters providing opportunities for reforming and reassembling these social and material networks of people, places, events and things into the future.

References

Basu, P. (2015). Reanimating cultural heritage: Digital curatorship, knowledge networks, and social transformation in Sierre Leone. In S. Macdonald & H. R. Leahy (Eds.), *The international handbooks of museum studies* (Vol. 4, pp. 337–364). Oxford: Wiley-Blackwell.

Bienkowski, P. (2015). A critique of museum restitution and repatriation practices. In S. Macdonald & H. R. Leahy (Eds.), *The international handbooks of museum studies* (Vol. 2, pp. 432–453). Oxford: Wiley-Blackwell.

Bohaker, H., Ojiig Corbiere, A., & Phillips, R. (2015). Wampum unites: Digital access, interdisciplinarity and indigenous knowledge – situating the GRASAC knowledge sharing database. In R. Silverman (Ed.), *Museum as process: Translating local and global knowledges* (pp. 45–66). London: Routledge.

Butts, D. (2007). Māori, museums and the Treaty of Waitangi: The changing politics of representation and control. In S. J. Knell, S. MacLeod, & S. Watson (Eds.), *Museum revolutions: How museums change and are changed* (pp. 215–227). London: Routledge.

Christen, K. (2015). Tribal archives, traditional knowledge, and local contexts: Why the "s" matters. *Journal of Western Archives*, *6*(1, Article 3), 1–19. Retrieved from http://digitalcommons.usu.edu/westernarchives/vol6/iss1/3.

Hakiwai, A. (1999). Kaitiakitanga – looking after the culture: Insights from "within" – two curatorial perspectives. *ICOM Ethnographic Conservation Newsletter*, *19*.

Horwood, M. (2017). Going digital in the GLAM sector: ICT innovations & collaborations for taonga Māori. In H. Whaanga, M. Apperley, & T. T. Keegan (Eds.), *Te whare hangarau Māori: Language, culture and technology* (pp. 149–164). Hamilton: University of Waikato.

Lythberg, B., Hogsden, C., & Ngata, W. (2017). Relational systems and ancient futures: Co-creating a digital contact network in theory and practice. In B. Onciul, M. L. Stefano, & S. Hawke (Eds.), *Engaging heritage, engaging communities* (Vol. Heritage Matters, pp. 205–226). Woodbridge: Boydell Press.

Mallon, S., Kanawa, R. T., Collinge, R., Balram, N., Hutton, G., Carkeek, T. W., Hakiwai, A., Case, C., Aipa, K., & Kapeliela, K. (2017). The 'ahu 'ula and mahiole of Kalaniʻōpuʻu: A journey of chiefly adornments. *Tuhinga*, *28*(4–23).

Matai Edmunds, B. (2018). *Untangling the threads*. Retrieved from http://www.aucklandmuseum.com/discover/stories/blog/2018/untangling-the-threads.

McCarthy, C. (2011). *Museums and Maori: Heritage professionals, indigenous collections, current practice*. Wellington: Te Papa Press.

O'Donovan, M., & Richardson, Z. (2017). Navigating good practice image permissions for Māori collections held at Auckland War Memorial Museum – Tāmaki Paenga Hira. In H. Whaanga, T. T. Keegan, & M. Apperley (Eds.), *He whare hangarau Māori: Language, culture & technology* (pp. 165–177). Hamilton: University of Waikato.

Silverman, R. (2015). *Museum as process: Translating local and global knowledges*. London: Routledge.

Glossary

hapū descent group, sub-tribe
hoeroa long whalebone weapon and ceremonial staff
hui meeting, assembly, coming together
iwi group of people bound together by descent from a common ancestor or ancestors, tribe
kaitiaki (kaitiakitanga) guardian, to care for, look after; guardianship
kapa haka dance performance
kōrero to tell, speak, talk
kuia respected female elder
mana ancestral authority, power, prestige
Mana Taonga principle defines Māori participation and involvement at Te Papa through recognising the spiritual and cultural connections of taonga with their people through whakapapa
manaaki (manaakitanga) to care for, look after, show respect, kindness, hospitality
Māori indigenous New Zealander
marae complex of buildings around the courtyard and meeting house for a hapū or iwi, settlement
mauri life-force, life-giving essence or principle
pā fortified refuge or settlement
Pākehā New Zealander of European descent
rangatira (rangatiratanga) chief, leader of a tribe; chiefly authority
taiaha long weapon and ceremonial staff
tangata whenua literally people of the land
tangata tiriti literally people of the Treaty, or New Zealanders of non-Māori origin
taonga treasured possession; in the Māori world view, taonga are seen as ancestors, living embodiments of whakapapa
tapu sacred, under ancestral restriction

tikanga   correct procedure, customary system of values and practices deeply embedded in the social context

waiata   song, chant, poetry

waka   canoe

whakapapa   genealogy, kinship, relationships

whānau   extended family group; modern meaning is family

whanaunga (whanaungatanga)   relative; relationship, sense of family connection

Index

For Product Safety Concerns and Information please contact our EU
representative GPSR@taylorandfrancis.com
Taylor & Francis Verlag GmbH, Kaufingerstraße 24, 80331 München, Germany